# FORTUNE TELLING

HOW TO PREDICT YOUR OWN FUTURE

★ CHRIS MORGAN ★

# FORTUNE TELLING
## HOW TO PREDICT YOUR OWN FUTURE
### CHRIS MORGAN

Crescent Books
New York/Avenel, New Jersey

A QUINTET BOOK

This 1992 edition published by
Crescent Books, distributed by
Outlet Book Company Inc.,
a Random House Company,
40 Engelhard Avenue, Avenel, New Jersey 07001

Printed and bound in Singapore

ISBN 0-517-07311-0

8 7 6 5 4 3 2 1

This book was designed and produced by
Quintet Publishing Limited
6 Blundell Street
London N7 9BH

Creative Director: Richard Dewing
Designer: Chris Dymond
Project Editor: William Hemsley

Typeset in Great Britain by
Context Typesetting, Brighton
Manufactured in Singapore by Bright Arts (S) Pte Ltd
Printed in Singapore by Star Standard Industries (Pte) Ltd

# CONTENTS

# INTRODUCTION

There is a fascination with the future which draws most people – young and old, male and female, of every colour and belief – into spending some time and money on trying to discover what is going to happen to them, or what decisions they should make. (In Christian countries this is despite clear warnings against fortune-telling in the Bible, which says. for example, "Do not practise divination or sorcery." *Leviticus* 19: 6).

You are one of those people, or else you would not be reading this book. You probably do not know a great deal about the different methods of fortune telling (or divination). You could consult a professional who might give you a tarot reading, scrutinize your palm, cast your birth chart or look into a crystal ball for symbols of your future. Or, instead, you might be able to predict the future for yourself, and this book will teach you something about the current methods of fortune telling. It sets out a range of possibilities. In some cases it will give you enough information for you to try the system for yourself, at home. In other cases, where the method is very complicated or requires expensive equipment or a particular talent, it will help you to understand what is involved in the method.

Fortune telling has an extremely long history – longer than any written records show. Hundreds of methods have been used and discarded over the centuries. For example, it is rare these days for anybody to kill an animal in order to read fortunes from its still-warm entrails. Such methods are ignored here. This book will concentrate on the eleven major and a few minor methods still widely used in the West today.

## DINNER PARTY FORTUNE TELLING

Some minor methods are easily overlooked, or else are not thought of as "proper" fortune telling. For example, there are fortune cookies, common in American Chinese restaurants but rare in British Chinese restaurants. These are small pastry cases, folded over and cooked hard, each containing a strip of paper bearing a one-line homily or piece of advice, rather than an actual predictive fortune. Examples of such fortune-cookie slips are "Be on the alert for new opportunities" and "Proceed with caution". Obviously, nobody is meant to take the advice in fortune cookies very seriously.

A fortune-telling system need not be difficult or complex or take much time. It takes only a second to pull a fortune out of a fortune cookie. It takes only slightly longer to carry out some of the methods involving candles. The simplest is really just an omen. At a dinner party or similar gatherings where several people are sitting round a table, light a new candle and place it in the centre. Note which side the molten wax first begins to run down, because it signifies bad luck for the person sitting at that side of the table. Slightly more formal, and requiring some preparation, are two other candle methods, lithomancy and lychnomancy. (The word-ending "-mancy" means "fortune telling by means of".) "Litho-" comes from "*lithos*", the ancient Greek word for a stone, while "lycho-" comes from "*lynchnos*", the Greek for a lamp.

7

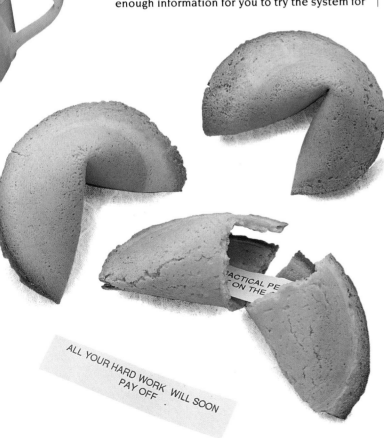

ALL YOUR HARD WORK WILL SOON PAY OFF .

ACTICAL PE ON THE

8

## LYCHNOMANCY

Set up three ordinary wax candles in a triangle, preferably in three identical candlesticks or holders. This should be done in a room with its doors and windows closed and no draughts to affect the burning of flames. Then turn off all other lights in the room (you will need a small torch or perhaps another candle, already lit, to see your way) and light the three candles with the same match. Clues to the future can be read in the behaviour of the candle flames.

- If one candle seems to burn more brightly than the other two it means success and good fortune for you.

- If the end of any of the three wicks displays a brightly shining point it is a lucky omen.
- If a flame moves from side to side it indicates that you will soon travel.
- If there are sparks rising from a candle you will need to be cautious.
- If the flame of one of the candles seems to twist and spiral it means that your enemies are plotting against you.
- If a flame rises and falls it suggests there is approaching danger.
- If one of the candles is extinguished suddenly and without good reason it is a prediction of great disaster.

### LITHOMANCY

Scatter a few precious or semi-precious stones on a flat surface – they must be of a variety of colours. Light a candle and set it up in the middle of them. Turn off all other lights to aid your concentration and close your eyes. When you open them, note the colour of the first stone which catches your eye by reflecting the candle light towards you.

A blue stone means good luck; a colourless one, happiness and success; green means a wish granted; red means romance; claret means a marriage; turquoise indicates an opportunity; yellow means unfaithfulness; grey is for sadness; violet for grief: purple for a quarrel and black for bad luck.

# REINVENTED FORTUNE TELLING METHODS

It is interesting to note how many new fortune-telling systems or devices have appeared for sale over the last five years or so. Some are old methods reinvented, such as rune stone (see page 10). Others are brand new in the way they are marketed and presented, though in essence they are just slight variations of age-old methods. Included in this category are sets of fortune-telling cards which are neither tarot packs nor standard playing cards, but something gimmicky which is probably less versatile than either. They are widely available, but this book deliberately ignores them.

# RUNES

About 1,800 years ago the runic alphabet came into being among the Norse peoples of northern Europe. It was said to be a gift from Odin, chief of the Norse gods. One of its uses was as a predictive device, carefully controlled by rune masters. The last rune masters lived in Iceland in the seventeenth century, and it was only about ten years ago that runes were reintroduced for divination.

Although slight variations exist, the sets of runes on sale today are fairly traditional. Sets consists of 25 rune stones (occasionally only 22). Each, except for a blank, is marked with a symbol of the runic alphabet, made up of straight lines because it was easier to carve straight lines into stone rather than curves.

### RUNE POSITIONS

For reading purposes, the rune stones should be placed face down and shuffled, then thirteen chosen and arranged in a clock face, proceeding anticlockwise from 9 o'clock, with the thirteenth in the centre. These positions are concerned with:

| | | | |
|---|---|---|---|
| 1 | personality | 7 | love and marriage |
| 2 | material wealth | 8 | inheritance |
| 3 | family | 9 | education |
| 4 | home | 10 | job, status |
| 5 | self-expression | 11 | pleasures, |
| 6 | health and the | | friendship |
| | environment | 12 | psychic feelings |
| | | 13 | the questioner. |

Note that runes are upright if their tops are closest to the centre.

## RUNE MEANINGS

(**R** means that the rune is reversed or inverted)

**Feoh** property, wealth, fulfilment, growth. **R** loss.

**Ur** strength masculinity, skill. **R** weakness, missed chances.

**Thorn** protection of all kinds. **R** wrong decision, jealousy.

**Os** authority, father figures. **R** problems with superiors.

**Rad** movement, change. **R** problems with travel or changes.

**Ken** warmth, love, status. **R** lack of warmth or direction.

**Gyfu** gift, opportunity. **R** loss, swindle, illness.

**Wyn** joy, happiness, luck. **R** overemotion, depression.

**Hagal** sudden change, good or bad. **R** delay, disaster.

**Nyd** self-preservation, needs. **R** tension, stress.

**Is** obstacles, stagnation. **R** fear, coldness, no hope.

**Ger** end of a cycle, renewal **R** the same.

**Eoh** flexibility, cunning. **R** indecision, withdrawal.

**Peorth** occult knowledge, hope. **R** disappointment, fear.

**Eolhs** artistry, culture, pleasure. **R** a lack of these.

**Sygel** life force, healing, fame. **R** the same, overused.

**Tir** energy, heroism, romance. **R** weakness, love spurned.

**Beorc** fertility, beginnings. **R** barrenness, delay, illness.

**Eow** travel, animals, ideas. **R** problems with these.

**Man** authority, consult professionals. **R** trouble with these.

**Lagu** intuition, change, fertility. **R** paranoia, blood.

**Ing** fertility, fruition, solution. **R** restriction, illness.

**Daeg** face values, clarity, success. **R** the same.

**Ethel** legacy, gift, help. problems with property.

**The blank rune** fate, hidden things; its meaning is partly determined by adjacent runes.

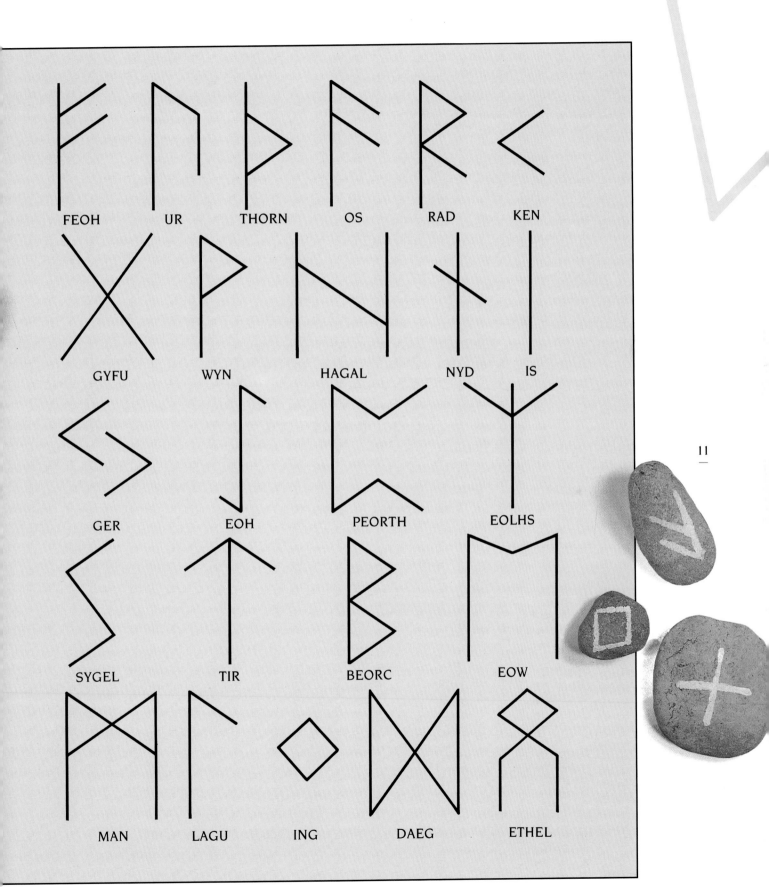

FEOH      UR      THORN      OS      RAD      KEN

GYFU      WYN      HAGAL      NYD      IS

GER      EOH      PEORTH      EOLHS

SYGEL      TIR      BEORC      EOW

MAN      LAGU      ING      DAEG      ETHEL

11

CHAPTER 1

# WESTERN ASTROLOGY

*Quite complex tables and an ephemeris are needed to cast a horoscope.*

13

At the moment of your birth, the Sun, Moon and eight planets were at precise positions in the sky. They were in the same segments of the sky as various of the twelve particular constellations of stars which make up the Zodiac. The strengths and weaknesses of your personality and some of the major events in your life were predetermined by these astronomical positions. This is the basis of the complex science of astrology.

Of course, to most people, astrology means the highly simplified populist approach of those newspapers and magazines that feature an astrology column. This very general forecast is based solely on the stellar position of the Sun on the day of your birth and it is unlikely to have much accuracy.

Somebody who says, "I'm a Taurus," or "I'm a Scorpio," is merely stating that the Sun was passing through the constellation of Taurus or Scorpio (respectively) when he or she was born. This is known as "Sun-sign astrology". It is used because it is simple. The fact that the Sun is in the same part of the sky on a particular date every year means that, whatever your age, if you were born between 21st April and 21st May, for example, your star sign is Taurus. A twelfth of the world's population has the same Sun sign as you. Sun-sign astrology has limited accuracy.

# THE ZODIAC

The Zodiac is a relatively narrow band of stars (about 18° wide) against which the Sun, Moon and planets move. It stretches right round the Earth and its 360° have been divided up into twelve equal segments of 30°. These segments are named after twelve constellations of stars that more or less occupy parts of the segments. The constellations correspond to the twelve signs of the Zodiac. Note that the central line of the Zodiac is known as the ecliptic.

This idea of a Zodiac is very ancient – dating back as far as the time of the Babylonians, about 4,000 years ago. The Babylonians, who were relatively advanced in the studies of mathematics and astronomy developed the basis of a system of divination that studied the influence of the Sun, Moon, planets and stars.

# A SHORT HISTORY OF WESTERN ASTROLOGY

It is important to remember that astrology was the same thing as astronomy for thousands of years, from Babylonian times through the refinement of techniques by the Greeks, Romans and early-medieval Arabs. The early Christians, especially St Augustine, attacked astrology, and it was in decline in Western Europe for about 800 years until the thirteenth century, when it saw some revival.

14

*Two fifteenth-century Zodiacs, arranged concentrically.*

Only in the seventeenth centry, when the first modern astronomers appeared, did astronomy split away from astrology. At the same time, there was increased interest in astrology, especially in England, and much of the complex detail was worked out by men such as John Dee (astrologer to Queen Elizabeth I); William Lilly, who in 1648 in his *Astrological Predictions* forecast "sundry fires and consuming plague" for London in about 1665 (he was correct, since the Great Plague was in 1665 and the Fire of London in 1666); Francis Moore (whose *Vox Stellarum* was an important early almanac, which became *Old Moore's Almanac*, still published each year); and Ebenezer Sibley who, in 1784, produced *The Celestial Art of Astrology*, the most complete and ambitious work on the subject up to that date.

Until 1931, astrological prediction had tended to be based on personal horoscopes (a horoscope is an astrological birth chart, showing the sky at the moment of birth, with the Earth in the centre surrounded by the planets and then the constellations). These were calculated individually and were quite difficult to produce. Essentially, they were private, produced by an astrologer for a client, and were not revealed to anybody else. But on August 24, 1931, Princess Margaret was born to the Duke and Duchess of York. (He was later King George VI; she is now the Queen Mother). *The Sunday Express* commissioned a birth chart of the baby and published it. This led to a sudden rekindling of interest in astrological predictions in several newspapers as a regular feature.

## CALCULATING A PERSONAL BIRTH CHART

It is a complex task to calculate a personal birth chart (the technical term is to erect or cast it). Only a brief outline as to the procedure will be given here so that you can appreciate some of the difficulties involved.

The basic equipment needed is a pair of compasses, a pencil, a protractor, an atlas that lists latitudes and longitudes of places around the world and (the difficult part) an ephemeris, which is a book giving the positions of the Sun, Moon and planets at particular times.

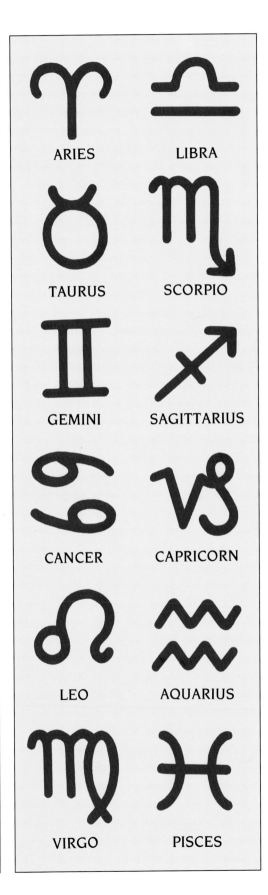

ARIES

LIBRA

TAURUS

SCORPIO

GEMINI

SAGITTARIUS

CANCER

CAPRICORN

LEO

AQUARIUS

VIRGO

PISCES

15

Ideally, you should draw two separate discs, one of which fits around the other. The outer disc (diagram 1) needs to be divided into 30°-segments inscribed with the twelve signs of the zodiac, proceeding anticlockwise from Aries through to Pisces. The inner disc (diagram 2) has the Earth at its centre. It is really a diagram of the sky, showing north, south, east and west, but reversed from normal maps, with east to the left. Also, it shows times, with dawn (6 am) to the east (this is known as the ascendant and is very important), noon to the south (at the top of the diagram, a position also known as Medium Coeli or Midheaven), dusk to the west and midnight (Immum Coeli) to the north.

Another feature of the basic diagram is the array of houses (diagram 3). These have no astronomical significance but are important in the analysis of fortune from the chart. There are twelve houses, arranged around the inner ring, going anticlockwise from the ascendant.

The divisions between the houses and between the zodiacal signs are known as cusps. The

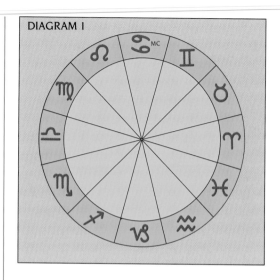

DIAGRAM 1

cusp of a particular house or sign is at its starting point. So the cusp of the first house is on the ascendant. House and sign cusps will not usually coincide. Cusps are important, because a planet close to one will be affected by the houses or signs to either side of the cusp, and so any prediction needs to be amended.

16

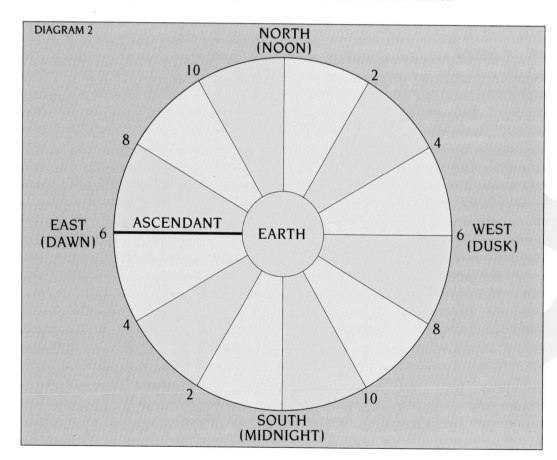

DIAGRAM 2

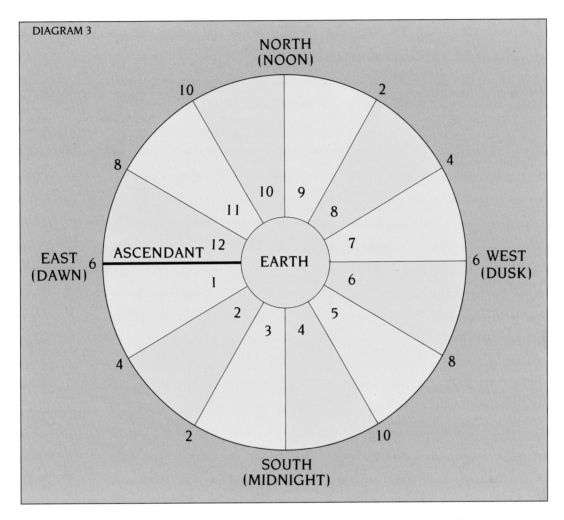

DIAGRAM 3

NORTH
(NOON)

EAST
(DAWN)

ASCENDANT

EARTH

WEST
(DUSK)

SOUTH
(MIDNIGHT)

To illustrate some of the particular difficulties of casting a birth chart, here are the time adjustments that need to be made. If you know your time of birth to the nearest minute you must then proceed as follows.

**A**  correct your time of birth to Greenwich Mean Time (GMT) by *adding* the time difference if you were born to the west of Greenwich (eg if you were born in New York, add five hours), or by *subtracting* the time difference if you were born to the east of Greenwich (eg if you were born in Queensland, Australia, subtract ten hours). If you were born in Britain or elsewhere on the Greenwich meridian, the GMT time zone covers you and no adjustment for longitude is necessary.

**B**  make an allowance for any daylight-saving time – that hour or occasionally more, by which some countries advance their clocks during the summer months.

**C**  consult an ephemeris to find the sidereal time by GMT at noon on the day of your birth. Sidereal times take account of the fact that the Earth rotates on its axis in a fraction less than 24 hours. If you were born after noon you need to add (or if before noon subtract) a further allowance.

**D**  having found the exact sidereal time of your birth, you can now look up the positions of the Sun, Moon and planets at that time (or adjust it from noon data). You will be able to set the ascendant on your birth chart to the correct number of degrees of the correct sign, then fasten the two separate discs together and fill in the rest of the data.

If all this sounds like too much trouble, there is now a large range of computer software available to do the job for you. All you need to do is to feed in your longitude of birth and the local time when you were born.

# HOUSES

**Each of the twelve houses is connected with a specific area of the individual's life for prediction purposes.**

## FIRST HOUSE

Strongly concerned with the self, this house shows how the person presents his or her personality to the world. There are connections, too, with childhood, with development and with any new beginning. The ascending sign will always tend to dominate this house, though there is also a connection with the sign of Aries and the planet Mars. Any planet that transits this house is likely to set off some new trend in the person's life.

## SECOND HOUSE

This house is connected strongly with possessions, including money, goods, property and even the prospects for earning or accumulating more money. Personal security is part of this, too. The person's capabilities (including artistic ones) are included. There are connections with the sign of Taurus and the planet Venus.

## THIRD HOUSE

The subjects concerning this house pertain to communications, the relationship of the individual to the nearby environment via letters, phone calls and short journeys. Family, neighbours and acquaintances are frequently involved, though business relationships might be included. Everyday contact with others is important. The sign connected with the third house is Gemini and the planet Mercury.

## FOURTH HOUSE

The home and domestic life are the subjects here, though one's original home and roots may be included. By extension, anything in this house may affect the property in which the subject lives, or those with whom he or she lives, or even somebody (like a mother) who was important during his or her formative years. The sign is Cancer and the planet is Mars.

## FIFTH HOUSE

This is the "fun" house. It is connected with leisure pursuits of all kinds – hobbies, sports, the arts, holidays – that can allow self-expression and bring happiness. Lovemaking is influenced by this house, as are pregnancy and children. ("Children" can also be taken to mean one's ideas, plans and non-living creations.) The Sun and sign of Leo are associated here.

## SIXTH HOUSE

This house concerns the subject's role in the community, including relationships with superiors and subordinates. Service is the keyword here, whether it is at work, in the house or elsewhere in society. Another area covered is personal health (or illness), doctors and hospitals, and also nutrition and wholesomeness. Virgo is the sign and Mercury the planet.

## SEVENTH HOUSE

This is the domain of important personal relationships, especially with one's life partner, business partners and any other relationships which require co-operation. The focus is on other people and there are indications of which types the subject is best suited to (though enemies and competitors are also included). The sign is Libra and the planet Venus.

## EIGHTH HOUSE

The emphasis here is on sharing, particularly money and personal possessions. So any money matters which involve others (wills, taxes, one's partners income and assets) are included. So, too, are sexual relationships, shared feelings and any kind of beginning or ending, such as birth, death and great changes in outlook or lifestyle. The sign is Scorpio and the planet may be Pluto or Mars.

## NINTH HOUSE

The expansion of horizons is covered here, literally in terms of travel to distant places or communication with them, metaphorically through further education, and spiritually through religion or philosophy. Relationships with foreigners are included, though these may just be non-blood relatives. Whatever else, a mental expansion is generally involved. The sign is Sagittarius and the planet is Jupiter.

## TENTH HOUSE

The subject's career, status and goals are connected with this house. The ego is at the centre of it, and how well any ambitions are achieved or frustrated – not just in one's career but also in, for example, politics or creative pursuits. Authority figures and organizations are important here, and one's relationships with and in them. The sign connected with this house is Capricorn and the planet Saturn.

## ELEVENTH HOUSE

Friendships and group activities are central in this house, though more in the realm of hobbies and pastimes than at work. There can still be hopes and ambitions involved, but these are as much for the group as for oneself. All kinds of learning (though mostly for pleasure) are included. Some unconventional or eccentric activities could be involved. Aquarius is the sign and Saturn or Uranus the planet.

## TWELFTH HOUSE

This is the house concerned with solitariness – one's inner feelings, worries, psychological sufferings and doubts. It is full of negative influences, often prophesying ill health and weakness, although some positive influences, such as self-sacrifice, secret love and hidden talent are included. It is the place of illusions, day-dreams and exclusion from normal life. Pisces is the sign and Neptune or Jupiter the planet.

19

# PLANETS

The original seven "planets" of the ancients were the Sun, the Moon (neither of which is actually a planet, of course), Mercury, Venus, Mars, Jupiter and Saturn, all of which were visible to the naked eye. The word planet comes from the Greek *planetes*, meaning wanderer, because these heavenly bodies appeared to the ancients to be wandering about against the fixed backcloth of stars.

Since the invention of the telescope, the other three planets of our solar system, Uranus, Neptune and Pluto, have been discovered, although these are so distant and take so long to move through their orbits that their effect upon any astrological predictions is small.

Each of the planets has certain characteristics attached to it, which vary a little according to the Zodiacal sign in which that planet was at the subject's birth or will be in the near future. These characteristics and the prospects associated with them will be modified again according to which of the houses that planet is in (or was in at the subject's birth, or is moving into during a future period which is being predicted). This kind of analysis is the stuff of which astrological prediction is made.

20

*The 12 signs of the Zodiac from an early sixteenth century calendar.*

## THE SUN

As the source of life and the "father" of the family of planets, the Sun has the most powerful influence upon the personality. It represents self-integration, authority and vitality. It rules the heart and the spine. As a powerful "masculine" force, it may be seen as governing the creative and generative power of man; for a woman it represents power and career prospects and also the men in her life. The good side of the Sun's influence is leadership; the bad side is arrogance and intolerance.

The Sun influences the signs that it passes through as follows:

**Aries** enterprising, enjoying control; perhaps opinionated or confrontational.

**Taurus** persistent, resourceful; perhaps stubborn, a bad enemy.

**Gemini** versatile, communicative; could be vague or inconsistent.

**Cancer** imaginative, shrewd, home-loving; may be shy or self-pitying.

**Leo** (the Sun's own sign) powerful confident, dignified; or boastful and attention-seeking.

**Virgo** thoughtful, modest, efficient; may be fussy or interfering.

**Libra** easy-going, diplomatic and friendly; perhaps indecisive or lazy; may lack confidence.

**Scorpio** passionate, secretive, determined; may be jealous or brooding.

**Sagittarius** optimistic, enthusiastic, tolerant, loving freedom; or extravagant and restless.

**Capricorn** practical, serious, hard-working; may be reserved, selfish.

**Aquarius** independent, idealistic; perhaps rebellious, too unconventional.

**Pisces** Sympathetic, kind, emotional; but impractical, secretive, timid.

## THE MOON

With its "female" qualities, the Moon represents the response to life – the moods. The Moon controls the qualities of intuition, affection and spirituality. Because the Moon is associated with water through its influence on the tides, it stands for changes, motions and rhythms, including pregnancy and the physical changes of life. Each time the Moon is full or new it has an effect on one's fortunes, and the occasional eclipses (every few months) are significant. It rules the stomach, breasts, ovaries and digestive system. The bad features of the Moon are moodiness, impulsiveness and a tendency excessive passivity.

The Moon and all the other planets are affected by their passage through the signs of the zodiac, as the Sun is, but this introductory guide will not list them all.

## MERCURY

As the messenger of the gods in Roman mythology, it is no surprise to find that this planet's main astrological symbolism is communication. To be mercurial is to be bright, witty, volatile and physically and mentally agile; and so it is with people born under Mercury. The head rules the heart here. And Mercury is concerned with the nervous system, brain, lungs and thyroid. There is an association, too, with childhood and youth (because Mercury is the smallest of the plants) and with education. On the negative side are tendencies towards impetuousness and irrational moods; Mercury is also something of a trickster.

## VENUS

This very female planet is concerned with harmony and unity. Although Venus stands for friendship and love, the connection with unbridled sexual passion is often overstated. The love of beauty, elegance, artistry and peace are Venusian traits. A man born under Venus may perhaps be controlled by a woman. The throat, kidneys and parathyroid glands are Venus's concern. The negative qualities include tendencies towards weakness, shyness and passivity in both men and women.

## MARS

An active, energetic, healthy character, full of male passions. Not necessarily warlike, despite tradition, although perhaps possessing a quick temper. Other traits are fearlessness, tenacity and straightforwardness. Perhaps too aggressive and shallow. The sex glands, urinary system and kidneys are governed by Mars.

## JUPITER

This, the largest of the planets, symbolizes improvement, cheerfulness, optimism, expansion and broad-mindedness. Attitudes are mature, genererous and big-hearted, though moral and conservative. Affable and unselfish, seeking success but not materialistic, Jupiter represents mature middle-age. The negative

21

side includes conceit, exaggeration, perhaps even criminal activity. It controls the body's healing, the liver and pituitary gland.

## SATURN

Personified as an old man. Saturn's great strengths are responsibility and capability. The virtues of the Saturnian include caution, control, patience and thrift. It is an unhappy planet, bringing difficult circumstances, and, on its own, would be a bad influence in anybody's horoscope. There is a lack of humour, of happiness or of any real emotion. The body's skin, bones and teeth are ruled by Saturn.

## URANUS

Representing change, freedom and originality, Uranus has an uncertain effect upon horoscopes. Despite its great distance from Earth, it spends seven years in each sign, and therefore it is a little more influential that might be supposed. Even so, some astrologers ignore its influence. There is a certain mysticism and willingness to behave out of character associated with Uranus subjects. Uranus controls the circulatory system and the pineal gland.

## NEPTUNE

Even less signficant than Uranus, due to its greater distance and slower pace, Neptune is the mystic planet, standing for intuition and the imagination. Subjects possess great sensitivity, although they tend towards vagueness, chaos and self-destroying addictions. Neptune rules not only the waves but, in the human body, the spine, parts of the nervous system and the thalamus. It is a planet that has been in only some of the constellations this century.

## PLUTO

The planet of the unknown and the unconscious, Pluto stands for transformation. Its subjects are individualists. Its effects need to be faced alone. Pluto controls the reproductive system, and it is associated with beginnings and endings (birth and death). Only a few signs this century have been affected by it.

# ELECTIONAL ASTROLOGY

A different approach to astrological forecasting is not to make predictions based on a particular existing birth date, but to select a lucky birth date in advance. Not for babies, this is for ceremonies or starting points. Among Far Eastern societies it has long been the custom to choose an auspicious day for a wedding, using planetary positions.

Although such beliefs have been largely suppressed in communist China, Chinese communities in Hong Kong, the US, Britain and elsewhere still keep to the tradition. In fact, it is a practice that is spreading into business, with firms opening, projects beginning or contracts being signed on astrologically-forecast days which will bring luck to the enterprise.

A good early example of electional astrology was when John Flamstead, Britain's first Astronomer Royal, selected the precise lucky time for founding the Greenwich observatory – at 3:14 in the afternoon of August 10, 1675.

23

## DIANA, PRINCESS OF WALES

Lady Diana is a complex Cancerian subject. Naturally a shy and sensitive type, as are Cancerians, she has been forced by her marriage to Prince Charles into becoming a world-famous celebrity, the centre of attention wherever she goes. Only a tough "survivor" type of person could have coped. She has had to change, and she has been helped in this by her ascendant, Saggitarius. This has given her the friendly, extrovert, approach to her royal duties that has endeared her to the crowds. At the same time, it has meant that she never quite conforms; at least, not all the time. She takes her sense of fun with her and is likely to do something unpredictable; not outrageous, but just to behave in a refreshingly light-hearted manner. Even the occasional wink or giggle is enough to help her cope with the sober protocol of royal occasions.

The other cause of her slightly unconventional approach to life is her Moon in Aquarius, giving a restlessness and an inquisitive nature.

Cancerians are noted for their home-loving personalities and maternal instincts, and in this respect Lady Diana is obviously typical. She is tremendously fond of children and very protective of her family and home.

# CHAPTER 2

# CHINESE ASTROLOGY

This book was written in the year of the Goat and published in the year of the Monkey. Only a decade ago, that statement would not have been understood by most people in the West. But the Chinese astrological system of animal years has achieved such a high profile during the last few years, with many books published on the subject and features appearing in major magazines on the occasion of each Chinese New Year, that there can be few people still unaware of it.

There are twelve animal year-signs, following each other in a regular cycle. For example, 1991 was the year of the Goat. So was 1979 and before that 1967. The next year of the Goat will be 2003.

A small complication is that the Chinese astrological years do not correspond exactly to our calendar years because they are based on the lunar cycle. The Chinese New Year is on a different date each year.

The twelve animals in the cycle are (in order) the Rat, the Buffalo or Ox, the Tiger, the Cat or Rabbit or Hare, the Dragon, the Snake, the Horse, the Goat, the Monkey, the Rooster or Cockerel, the Dog, and the Pig or Boar.

It is important to realize that there is no connection between Chinese astrology and Western astrology. No correspondence exists between the twelve animals and the twelve signs of the zodiac.

It must also be pointed out that the animal signs are what Chinese astrology is best known for, they are only a small and relatively unimportant part of a very complex area of divination. Your month, day and hour of birth can be integrated into a much more accurate assessment of your fortunes.

The basis of the Chinese animal system is that people born in a particular year are likely to possess particular personality characteristics. So a person born in 1960 (the year of the Rat) will be different from a person born in 1959 (the year of the Pig) or 1961 (the year of the Buffalo), but will tend to have some similarities with a person born in 1948 or 1972 (also years of the Rat). This is greatly simplifying the system; in fact there are subtle differences between people born in different years carrying the same sign.

## THE RAT

| | | |
|---|---|---|
| Jan 31, 1900 | to | Feb 19, 1901 |
| Feb 18, 1912 | to | Feb 6, 1913 |
| Feb 5, 1924 | to | Jan 25, 1925 |
| Jan 24, 1936 | to | Feb 11, 1937 |
| Feb 10, 1948 | to | Jan 29, 1949 |
| Jan 28, 1960 | to | Feb 15, 1961 |
| Feb 15, 1972 | to | Feb 3, 1973 |
| Feb 2, 1984 | to | Feb 20 1985 |

26

### RAT CHARACTERISTICS

Rats are often opportunists, with charm and tenacity. They are ambitious, often greedy. You will find them in company (for they tend not to be loners) but you may find them arriving late, as punctuality is not one of their strengths. Rats dislike routine work and are often to be found in jobs or professions where each day brings something new.

**In love**, the Rat is most compatible with other Rats and very compatible with Buffaloes, Dragons or Monkeys, but not get on well at all with Goats or Roosters.

**In marriage**, the Rat should go for a Dragon, or perhaps a Goat or Pig, and certainly not a Tiger, Cat or Horse.

**In business**, the spouse could also be the ideal business partner, for here, too, the Dragon is the best bet.

### FAMOUS RATS

George Bush, Joan Collins, Ivan Lendl, Prince Charles, William Shakespeare and Mozart.

*Prince Charles*

## THE BUFFALO

| | | |
|---|---|---|
| **Feb 19, 1901** | to | **Feb 7, 1902** |
| **Feb 6, 1913** | to | **Jan 25, 1914** |
| **Jan 25, 1925** | to | **Feb 12, 1926** |
| **Feb 11, 1937** | to | **Jan 30, 1938** |
| **Jan 29, 1949** | to | **Feb 16, 1950** |
| **Feb 15, 1961** | to | **Feb 4, 1962** |
| **Feb 3, 1973** | to | **Jan 22, 1974** |
| **Feb 20, 1985** | to | **Feb 9, 1986** |

### BUFFALO CHARACTERISTICS

Buffaloes are hard-working, strong-minded and extremely punctual. They tend not to have close friends and often suffer problems in love and marriage. Continuity is important to them, and they dislike change or interruptions. You will find them in routine jobs everywhere, in which they are often highly valued.

**In love**, the Buffalo will relate well with a Rooster or a Pig and should not attempt a relationship with a Tiger or a Goat.

**In marriage**, only a Rooster is really compatible, since Buffaloes are often very difficult to live with; other Buffaloes, Tigers, Dragons, Horses and Dogs are best avoided.

**In business**, the Buffalo gets on best with a horse or a pig and not at all with a Tiger, Dragon, Snake, Goat, Monkey or Dog.

## FAMOUS BUFFALOES

Margaret Thatcher, Robert Redford, Princess Diana, Marlene Dietrich and Fidel Castro.

*Marlene Dietrich*

## THE TIGER

| | | |
|---|---|---|
| Feb 8, 1902 | to | Jan 28, 1903 |
| Jan 26, 1914 | to | Feb 13, 1915 |
| Feb 13, 1926 | to | Feb 1, 1927 |
| Jan 31, 1938 | to | Feb 18, 1939 |
| Feb 17, 1950 | to | Feb 5, 1951 |
| Feb 5, 1962 | to | Jan 24, 1963 |
| Jan 23, 1974 | to | Feb 10, 1975 |
| Feb 9, 1986 | to | Jan 29, 1987 |

28

### TIGER CHARACTERISTICS

Tigers are dynamic, "ideas" people, liable to become impatient, to quarrel, to complain loudly and to be noticed wherever they are. They can be elegant and flamboyant. Their lives are often unpredictable, with violent ups and downs. They lack endurance and often make changes just for the sake of it.

**In love**, the Tiger has great compatibility with the Dragon and only slightly less with the Horse; Buffaloes, Snakes and other Tigers are worth a Tiger's while avoiding.

**In marriage**, a Dog is the best partner, or perhaps a Dragon or a Pig; but a Tiger should not marry a Rat, Buffalo or Snake.

**In business**, the Tiger will do very well with either Dragons or Horses and should not get mixed up with Buffaloes, other Tigers, Snakes, Roosters or Dogs.

### FAMOUS TIGERS

Marilyn Monroe was an archetypal Tiger. Others are Sir Alec Guinness and Queen Elizabeth II.

*Marilyn Monroe*

# THE CAT

| | | |
|---|---|---|
| **Jan 29, 1903** | to | **Feb 15, 1904** |
| **Feb 14, 1915** | to | **Feb 2, 1916** |
| **Feb 2, 1927** | to | **Jan 22, 1928** |
| **Feb 19, 1939** | to | **Feb 7, 1940** |
| **Feb 6, 1951** | to | **Feb 26, 1952** |
| **Jan 25, 1963** | to | **Feb 12, 1964** |
| **Feb 11, 1975** | to | **Jan 30, 1976** |
| **Jan 29, 1987** | to | **Feb 28, 1988** |

## CAT CHARACTERISTICS

Cats are sensitive and good listeners. Push them hard and you should get what you want. They like a quiet life (especially at home) and try to avoid strong emotions of any kind. A Cat is likely to be methodical in all things, light-hearted and not very deep thinkers, cats are good to have around – they are often very popular.

**In love,** the Cat gets on perfectly with a Dragon, very well with a Horse, a Goat or another Cat, and fairly well with a Buffalo, a Snake, a Monkey, a Dog and a Pig; only the Rooster is incompatible.

**In marriage,** the Cat is easy to please, and an ideal partner for a Dragon, a Snake, a Horse or another Cat; only a Rat or a Rooster should be avoided by a cat.

**In business,** the Cat has plenty of scope: is best with another Cat, highly compatible with a Rat, Dragon, Snake, Goat or Pig, and only in trouble when dealing with a Tiger or a Monkey.

## FAMOUS CATS

Bob Hope, Jodie Foster, David Frost and Queen Victoria.

29

*Bob Hope*

## THE DRAGON

| | | |
|---|---|---|
| Feb 16, 1904 | to | Feb 3, 1905 |
| Feb 3, 1916 | to | Jan 22, 1917 |
| Jan 23, 1928 | to | Feb 9, 1929 |
| Feb 8, 1940 | to | Jan 26, 1941 |
| Feb 27, 1952 | to | Feb 13, 1953 |
| Feb 13, 1964 | to | Feb 1, 1965 |
| Jan 31, 1976 | to | Feb 17, 1977 |
| Jan 17, 1988 | to | Jan 6, 1989 |

### DRAGON CHARACTERISTICS

A dragon tends to be a showperson, somewhat flashy and arrogant. The Dragon tends to be both admired and hated, with good friends and bad enemies. Like Buffaloes they hate routine. Dragons are mostly monogamous and loyal (although they need a good partner to look after them). They are often generous and almost invariably awkward.

**In love,** the dragon is superbly compatible with Tigers, Cats, Snakes, Horses and Monkeys and extremely good with Rats or Goats; only with Dogs or other Dragons are there likely to be serious problems.

**In marriage,** Dragons can similarly have great relationships with Rats, Monkeys or Roosters and pretty good ones with Tigers, Cats and Snakes; but Dragons must avoid other Dragons, Dogs and Buffaloes.

**In business,** Dragons do well with Rats, Tigers, Monkeys, Roosters or Pigs, but should beware of Buffaloes and Dogs.

### FAMOUS DRAGONS

Jeffrey Archer, Jimmy Connors, Shirley Temple and Cliff Richard.

*Jeffrey Archer*

# THE SNAKE

| | | |
|---|---|---|
| Feb 4, 1905 | to | Jan 24, 1906 |
| Jan 23, 1917 | to | Feb 10, 1918 |
| Feb 10, 1929 | to | Jan 29, 1930 |
| Jan 27, 1941 | to | Feb 14, 1942 |
| Feb 14, 1953 | to | Feb 2, 1954 |
| Feb 21, 1965 | to | Jan 20, 1966 |
| Feb 18, 1977 | to | Feb 6, 1978 |
| Feb 6, 1989, | to | Jan 27, 1990 |

## SNAKE CHARACTERISTICS

Snakes are wise and tenacious people, not necessarily beautiful but most often attractive. They tend towards infidelity but are also paradoxically very possessive. An artistic talent is a strong possibility, as is the ability to make money. Although preferring idleness and being prone to making wrong decisions, Snakes are good companions by virtue of their sense of humour, unwillingness to quarrel and ability to adapt to circumstances.

**In love**, the Snake is perfect for a Dragon, pretty good with a Horse and only incompatible with a Tiger or another Snake.

**In marriage**, the Snake has plenty of choice, though a Cat is best and a Tiger impossible.

**In business**, no relationships are perfectly smooth (they do best on their own) but they can manage with Cats.

## FAMOUS SNAKES

Bob Dylan, Placido Domingo and Lincoln.

31

*Placido Domingo*

## THE HORSE

32

| | | |
|---|---|---|
| Jan 25, 1906 | to | Feb 12, 1907 |
| Feb 11, 1918 | to | Jan 31, 1919 |
| Jan 30, 1930 | to | Feb 16, 1931 |
| Feb 15, 1942 | to | Feb 4, 1943 |
| Feb 3, 1954 | to | Jan 23, 1955 |
| Jan 21, 1966 | to | Feb 8, 1967 |
| Feb 7, 1978 | to | Jan 27, 1979 |
| Jan 27, 1990 | to | Feb 15, 1991 |

*Barbara Streisand*

## HORSE CHARACTERISTICS

Horses are elegant and easy-going with a good sense of humour. They may possess great sex appeal. Not that the social side is all they care about – they are often hard-workers, good decision-makers and natural leaders. They love company and are excellent listeners. Their only weaknesses are falling in love too easily and making changes too frequently.

**In love**, they are superbly compatible with Goats, Dogs and other Horses, pretty good with Tigers, Cats and Snakes but should avoid Monkeys, Roosters and Pigs.

**In marriage**, too, their choice is wide, with the Cat, Goat and another Horses being best, a Rooster or Dog very good, but never a Rat, Buffalo or Monkey.

**In business** a Horse should choose a Tiger or a Rooster as a business partner, though good results can be expected with a Buffalo, Cat, Dragon or Goat, but not with a Rat, a Pig or another Horse.

## FAMOUS HORSES

Muhammed Ali, Clint Eastwood and Barbara Streisand.

## THE GOAT

| | | |
|---|---|---|
| **Feb 13, 1907** | to | **Feb 1, 1908** |
| **Feb 1, 1919** | to | **Feb 19, 1920** |
| **Feb 17, 1931** | to | **Feb 5, 1932** |
| **Feb 5, 1943** | to | **Jan 24, 1944** |
| **Jan 24, 1955** | to | **Feb 11, 1956** |
| **Feb 9, 1967** | to | **Jan 29, 1968** |
| **Jan 28, 1979** | to | **Feb 15, 1980** |
| **Jan 17, 1988** | to | **Jan 6, 1989** |
| **Feb 16, 1991** | to | **Feb 3, 1992** |

### GOAT CHARACTERISTICS

A Goat enjoys life, but in his or her own way, preferably without restraints of any kind. Artistic and sociable. Goats are popular. They can also be fickle, insecure and bad at taking decisions. Not normally leaders, Goats are quite easily led or influenced by others.

**In love,** the Goat has little control and will do very well with a Horse or perhaps a Cat or a Dragon; but will not do well with a Rat, Buffalo, Rooster or Pig.

**In marriage,** the Horse is again best, and a Cat, Dragon or Pig can be quite compatible; Roosters and Dogs should be avoided.

**In business,** a Goat can get on quite well with a Cat, a Horse or as Pig, but will not get on at all with a Buffalo, a Rooster or a Dog.

## FAMOUS GOATS

Mikhail Gorbachev, Andy Warhol, John Major, Mick Jagger and Michelangelo.

*Andy Warhol*

33

## THE MONKEY

| | | |
|---|---|---|
| Feb 2, 1908 | to | Jan 21, 1909 |
| Feb 20, 1920 | to | Feb 7, 1921 |
| Feb 6, 1932 | to | Jan 25, 1933 |
| Jan 25, 1944 | to | Feb 12, 1945 |
| Feb 12, 1956 | to | Jan 30, 1957 |
| Jan 30, 1968 | to | Feb 16, 1969 |
| Feb 16, 1980 | to | Feb 4, 1981 |
| Feb 4, 1992 | to | Jan 23, 1993 |

34

### MONKEY CHARACTERTISTICS

The Monkey is a tricky person, quick, opportunistic, and often good with figures. He or she knows it, too, and is not modest. Monkeys have excellent memories and possess the potential to be very successful. Not succeeding would be due to impatience, superficiality and inability to share. At the same time, Monkeys can be generous and thoughtful people.

**In love**, the Monkey is highly compatible with Dragons, Pigs and other Monkeys, compatible with Rats and completely at odds with Horses or Dogs.

**In marriage**, it is very similar, with Dragons, Pigs and other Monkeys making ideal mates, Goats making good ones, and Horses or Roosters being the worst.

**In business**, the Monkey can work well in partnership with a Dragon or a Pig and not at all with a Buffalo, Cat, Rooster or Dog.

### FAMOUS MONKEYS

Michael Douglas, Elizabeth Taylor, Sebastion Coe, Ian Fleming and Diana Ross.

*Diana Ross*

# THE ROOSTER

| | | |
|---|---|---|
| Jan 22, 1909 | to | Feb 9, 1910 |
| Feb 8, 1921 | to | Jan 27, 1922 |
| Jan 26, 1933 | to | Feb 13, 1934 |
| Feb 13, 1945 | to | Feb 1, 1946 |
| Jan 31, 1957 | to | Feb 17, 1958 |
| Feb 17, 1969 | to | Feb 5, 1970 |
| Feb 5, 1981 | to | Jan 24, 1982 |
| Jan 23, 1993 | to | Feb 10, 1994 |

## ROOSTER CHARACTERISTICS

An honest and generous person, the Rooster offers your free advice whether you want it or not (though some Roosters are less extrovert). They can be either miserly or rash spenders. Almost always they are efficient, methodical people, though perhaps lacking in initiative.

**In love,** only the Buffalo is compatible, since Roosters are really interested in more permanent relationships.

**In marriage,** the Dragon is ideal, the Buffalo, Snake or Horse almost as good, while the Cat, Goat, Monkey or another Rooster are just impossible to live with.

**In business,** the Rooster gets on well with Dragons and Horses, slightly with Buffaloes and hardly at all with anyone else.

## FAMOUS ROOSTERS

Nick Faldo, Gloria Estefan, Eric Clapton and Errol Flynn.

*Nick Faldo*

35

*Michael Jackson*

# THE DOG

| | | |
|---|---|---|
| Feb 10, 1910 | to | Jan 29, 1911 |
| Jan 28, 1922 | to | Feb 15, 1923 |
| Feb 14, 1934 | to | Jan 23, 1935 |
| Feb 2, 1946 | to | Jan 21, 1947 |
| Feb 18, 1958 | to | Feb 7, 1959 |
| Feb 6, 1970 | to | Jan 26, 1971 |
| Jan 25, 1982 | to | Feb 12, 1983 |
| Feb 10, 1994 | to | Jan 31, 1995 |

## DOG CHARACTERISTICS

Dogs are hard-working people, loyal friends and can be great opponents of injustice. They may be stubborn or get bogged down with small details, and they do best as followers, not leaders. They have very high standards by which they judge themselves and those around them. They can be pessimistic.

**In love**, the Dog is wonderfully suited to a Horse or a Pig and not at all compatible with a Dragon or a Goat.

**In marriage**, a Tiger or a Pig is ideal; a Buffalo, Dragon or Goat is best avoided.

**In business**, only the pig will make a good partner; most other partnerships will not work.

## FAMOUS DOGS

Madonna, Uri Geller, Liza Minelli, Winston Churchill and Michael Jackson.

## THE PIG

In business, the Pig does best with a Monkey or a Dragon, and should avoid Horses.

| | | |
|---|---|---|
| **Jan 30, 1911** | to | **Feb 17, 1912** |
| **Feb 16, 1923** | to | **Feb 4, 1924** |
| **Feb 4, 1935** | to | **Jan 23, 1936** |
| **Jan 22, 1947** | to | **Feb 9, 1948** |
| **Feb 8, 1959** | to | **Jan 27, 1960** |
| **Jan 27, 1971** | to | **Jan 15, 1972** |
| **Feb 13, 1983** | to | **Feb 1, 1984** |
| **Jan 31, 1995** | to | **Feb 19, 1996** |

### FAMOUS PIGS

Woody Allen, Elton John and Maria Callas.

*Woody Allen*

### PIG CHARACTERISTICS

Pigs are very hardworkers and can be great moneymakers, especially as part of a team. They are open, straightforward people, strang-minded and self-confident without being cocky. Their generosity and steadfastness make them excellent friends. They can fall in love easily and take rejection very badly.

**In love,** the Pig is pretty compatible with any-one except a Horse, though especially suited to a Dog or another Pig.

**In marriage,** it's even better, ideal partners being Monkeys, Dogs or other Pigs, no signs being ruled out.

THE WORLD

THE SUN

THE WHEEL OF FORTUNE

# CHAPTER 3

# TAROT

TEMPERANCE

THE MOON

JUDGME

*There is a wide range of modern tarot card designs.*

The tarot resembles an enlarged pack of playing cards. In the standard tarot pack are 78 cards (as compared to 52 in a normal British or American pack of playing cards). Most of the extra cards are the trumps or Major Arcana. There are 22 of these, numbered 1 to 21, together with the Fool (not numbered but often thought of as number 0). The rest of the pack (the Minor Arcana) consists of four suites: swords, wands (sometimes known as rods, sceptres, staves or batons), cups and pentacles (also called coins or discs). Each suit has cards numbered familiarly from 1 to 10 and four court cards, the king, queen, knight and page.

## THE ORIGINS OF TAROT

Many different origins have been claimed for the tarot. It might be based on an ancient Egyptian book; it might be Indian, connected with a forerunner of the game of chess; it might have originally been Arabic, perhaps brought to Europe by returning crusaders; it might have travelled west from Asia to Europe with the movement of wandering gypsies. In fact, nobody knows for sure.

Originally, tarot cards were probably intended for several purposes. Certainly they were used as playing cards for a variety of games. They also seem to have been a representation of the period in pictures and symbols. For example, the four suits represent the division of society; swords for the military and nobility, cups (chalices) for the Church,

pentacles (coins) for the merchants and wands for the peasants. And the cards were also used to foretell the future.

There is a great deal of symbolism connected with the tarot, not all of it understood. It is certain that the Major Arcana have some link with the traditions of Hermetic magic and with Egyptian mythology. In particular there are strong connections between the tarot and an ancient Jewish tradition of mysticism, magic and astrology called the Kabbalah.

## MODERN DAY TAROT

Over the last fifteen years the tarot has been dramatically popularized. From being a scarce and rather esoteric fortune-telling device used by specialists and issued in a few packs with traditional designs, the tarot has become big business in the games and *objets d'art* markets. Dozens and dozens of newly designed packs have been marketed. Some have been showcases for the work of one or more artists. The surrealist, Salvador Dali illustrated a richly symbolic pack, using collage, as one of his last major works. Some have taken symbols from different mythological or cultural backgrounds, so that there are Celtic and Greek myth packs, a Japanese pack and an Amerindian pack. Others portray invented worlds, fantasy settings or futures. In addition, a few very early packs have been issued in restored form. Most of these packs are very beautiful, well worth seeing and eminently collectable. Many such packs are purchased and never used for fortune telling.

# THE MAJOR ARCANA

THE FOOL

### 0 THE FOOL

This is the only unnumbered card of the Major Arcana; it is generally regarded as card number 0, and is placed first. It has evolved into the Joker of the present day British and American pack of playing cards. A complex card, standing for many things one should avoid, including foolishness, thoughtlessness, recklessness; a lack of discipline or restraint; excessive behaviour, obsession or infatuation. It also stands for light-heartedness and pleasure. It is a warning to make the right choice in a vital matter rather than taking an easy way out. **R** a faulty choice or a lack of decision.

**R** indicates a reversed card (top to bottom).

THE MAGICIAN

### I THE MAGICIAN

A creative card; power, skill and trickery; determination to finish projects and to use one's own talents well. **R** lack of will; misuse of power; hesitation; ineptitude.

THE HIGH PRIESTESS

### 2 THE HIGH PRIESTESS

Wisdom and understanding; intuition; teaching; mystery, something hidden; serenity and an avoidance of emotional relationships. **R** superficiality, ignorance, poor judgment.

### 3   THE EMPRESS

Traditional "female" accomplishments, such as marriage, children, fertility, development, creativity, motivating others. **R** inaction, domestic problems, resources wasted.

### 5   THE HIEROPHANT (HIGH PRIEST)

Spiritual power, ritual; kind and merciful; conventional and conformist, even unwilling to change. Teacher or advisor. **R** unconventional, vulnerable, gullible.

41

### 4   THE EMPEROR

Traditional "male" success: power over others, leadership, wealth, strength, fatherhood; intelligence dominating emotion. **R** immaturity, lack of strength, lack of control.

### 6   THE LOVERS

The conflict or choice between flesh and spirit. Love relationships, romance, feelings; harmony and perfection. **R** wrong choice, interference, break-up of relationship.

### 7 THE CHARIOT

A contradictory card concerned with change and movement. Troubles and turmoil; problems overcome, success; progress; a journey. **R** sudden collapse, defeat, failure.

### 9 THE HERMIT

Wisdom, prudence; a movement towards spiritual goals. Also desertion, annulment, a person alone. **R** foolishness, a refusal to stop and think; immaturity.

42

### 8 JUSTICE

Justice, balance, reasonableness; the outcome will be fair; temptation is recognised and evil avoided. **R** injustice, the abuse of power, bigotry, misjudgement.

### 10 THE WHEEL OF FORTUNE

Unexpected good fortune; completion or solution; outcome for good or bad depending on adjacent cards; change and advancement. **R** bad luck, decline, interruption.

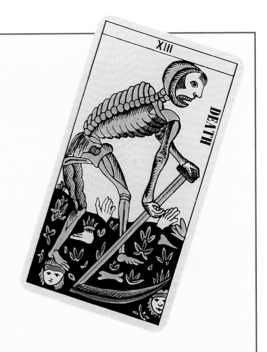

### 11   STRENGTH

Adversity is overcome by courage, strength, fortitude; physical ability; conquest of peril; love triumphs over hate. **R** weakness; obstacles not surmounted; lack of faith.

### 13   DEATH

Unexpected change, transformation; endings and beginnings for better or worse; illness; spiritual rebirth; progress from setbacks. **R** stagnation; destruction without renewal.

43

### 12   THE HANGED MAN

Change; decisions suspended for a while; sacrifice without immediate reward; rebirth and improvement coming. **R** rigid refusal to sacrifice oneself; lack of effort.

### 14   TEMPERANCE

A fortunate card exhorting moderation; patience and frugality; harmony between material and spiritual things. **R** lack of harmony; arguments, conflicts and hostilities.

### 15   THE DEVIL

Ominous events, including downfall, failure, subservience and bad influences; even death and disasters. Sexual temptation. **R** respite, release, spiritual enlightenment.

### 17   THE STAR

A fortunate card bringing bright prospects, hope, new opportunities, successful results from previous hard work. **R** lack of opportunity or success; hopes dashed; bad luck.

44

### 16   THE TOWER

Sudden and complete change. Everything is broken down, severed, disrupted, lost; but rebuilding can occur. **R** continuing in a rut, imprisonment (of any kind).

### 18   THE MOON

Beware of the trickery of others and deceptive circumstances; errors are likely; friends are false. An irritational card. **R** small problems, deceptions or mistakes are overcome.

### 19 THE SUN

Illumination, accomplishment; contentment from success, love, a happy marriage and simple everyday things. **R** loneliness, failure, hopes dashed, broken relationships.

### 21 THE WORLD

Change in the sense of completion; a triumphal result; goals achieved; the cycle ends to begin again; a very favourable card. **R** ultimate failure; lack of completion.

45

### 20 JUDGMENT

The weighing-up process of the Day of Judgement; spiritual development or rejuvenation. Review your conduct and atone if necessary. **R** regrets, delays, indecision.

It is important to undertstand that tarot divination is not simply a mechanical procedure of shuffling cards, laying a few out and reading their meanings from a book. There is a spiritual side to it, without which no accurate and helpful reading can be made.

The surroundings should be quiet and conducive to concentration. Probably the diviner and the subject will be alone together in a room, although public readings are occasionally given. The diviner must ensure that he or she is in the right mood for the reading and the subject must have some kind of question or problem in mind.

First (a step sometimes omitted) the diviner removes a court card from the pack to represent the subject. This is a wand if the subject has fair hair and blue eyes, a cup for light brown hair and palish eyes, a sword for dark brown hair and brown eyes and a pentacle for black hair and dark eyes. For a man as subject the king of the suit is selected, for a woman the queen, for a

## TAROT-READING TECHNIQUES

Divination with the tarot consists of the diviner spreading (the technical term for laying out, face up) a certain number of cards and interpreting their meanings. This is normally done in an attempt to answer a question or solve a problem put by the subject (or questioner), which may be voiced or not, as the subject wishes.

Very little of the fine detail of tarot divination is standard. There are many methods of operating and quite a number of different arrangements of the spread, using as few as seven cards (the Seven-Card Spread) or as many as 54 cards (the Royal Spread). The most commonly used today in Britain and America is the Celtic Method, a ten-card spread, which may be performed either from the whole pack or using just the Major Arcana.

THE CELTIC SPREAD

young man the knight and for a young women or child the page. The card, known as the significator, is placed face up on the table in front of the subject.

Then the diviner asks the subject to shuffle the pack. In fact, most diviners dislike anyone else handling their pack (they tend to keep it carefully wrapped in black silk and boxed to protect its vibrations) so the diviner may ask the subject only to cut the pack or perhaps just to place his or her hands on the pack for a moment while thinking about the question.

After shuffling, the pack is cut into three face-downward piles (usually by the subject) then picked up by the diviner. The top card is turned over and laid (face up) on top of the significator, covering it completely. The second card is turned over and laid across it. The next eight cards are turned over and laid down strictly in order (see illustration) to form a cross and then a line beside it.

## WHAT THE CARDS SIGNIFY

Each of these cards stand for some aspect of the subject's life and situation.

**Card 1** the present situation and general atmosphere.

**Card 2** the forces in opposition, obstacles.

**Card 3** the subject's hopes or goals.

**Card 4** distant past events or influences on which the present problem is based.

**Card 5** recent events, just past or still passing.

**Card 6** future influences.

Sometimes the diviner reads these six cards before turning over the next four.

**Card 7** the subject's present attitude or position regarding the problem.

**Card 8** those factors surrounding the subject which may be influential.

**Card 9** the subject's inner feelings on the problem.

**Card 10** the outcome.

If it should happen that more than half the cards are reversed (which radically alters their meaning), the reading cannot be trusted and these reversed cards must be turned upright.

Then the diviner speaks the reading aloud, interpreting each card for its personal symbolism and position.

Sometimes the answer ignores the question asked and penetrates to the heart of the real problem the subject has.

If the tenth card proves to be weak and unhelpful, a second reading may be done at once using that tenth card as the significator. The pack is shuffled, cut and laid out as before.

## A TAROT READING INTERPRETED

The significator was the King of Cups. The question asked was whether the questioner should persevere in his current job or try to find something different. The cards came out as follows.

**1 Two of Wands** (present position): uncertainty; great potential with some sadness indicated.

**2 Ace of Cups** immediate influences): good, on the questioner's side at present.

**3 The Magician** (hopes): self-confidence will provide the ability to succeed.

**4 The Fool reversed** (past influences): past decisions were foolish.

**5 Two of Swords** (influences still passing): the present is a peaceful hiatus in a discordant situation.

**6 Two of Pentacles reversed** (near-future influences): conflict and an irreconcilable situation.

**7 Seven of Swords** (questioner's attitude): mixed.

**8 Page of Cups** (environment, family and friends): help from a younger person, or the birth of an idea.

**9 Queen of Swords reversed** (hopes and fears): a bad female influence; negative feelings.

**10 The Wheel of Fortune** (outcome): constant change.

To summarize, this is a strong but mixed reading. It suggests that there are no magical solutions, but that if the questioner believes in himself and sticks at his current job he may do well, being helped by somebody else. Conflicts and changes are an almost inevitable part of life; they need to be accepted and coped with.

47

THE MAGICIAN

# THE MINOR ARCANA

## WANDS

**KING** an honest, mature person. Noble, loyal, conscientous, generally married. **R** severity. Advice to be taken.

**QUEEN** a sympathetic person. Loving, chaste, friendly. Success in business. **R** economical. Jealousy or deceit.

**KNIGHT** departure, a journey into the unknown. A young man creating rivalry. **R** discord, change, conflict.

**PAGE** a faithful young person. An envoy or messenger. Consistent, stable. **R** badness, indecision, reluctance.

**TEN** under excessive pressure; power used selfishly; problem soon solved. **R** difficulties, treachery, deceit.

**NINE** strength to face unexpected problems. Readiness. **R** obstacles, adversity.

**EIGHT** sudden progress, haste, perhaps a journey. Arrows of love. **R** jealousy, dispute, lack of harmony, quarrels.

**SEVEN** success over adversity through persistence. **R** anxiety, embarrassment, confusion.

**SIX** triumph, gain advancement, good news. **R** indefinite delay, fear, vulnerability.

**FIVE** struggle, stiff competition; some hope of general improvement. **R** complications, frustrations and contradictions.

**FOUR** romance, harmony, prosperity, peace. **R** the same.

**THREE** practical help in business; enterprise; strength. **R** beware of help. Treachery.

**TWO** mature ruler; boldness; success. **R** sadness. Troubles, misfortune.

**ONE** beginnings in the widest sense. Fortune. **R** false start, decadence.

## CUPS

**KING** a professional or business person, generous and responsible. **R** deceit and loss. Artistic temperament, unreliability.

**QUEEN** a good wife and mother, intuitive, practical; a visionary. **R** a good woman but inconsistent, untrustworthy, deceitful.

**KNIGHT** an invitation; advance or change; an intelligent messenger. **R** a subtle, sly, untrustworthy, deceitful person.

**PAGE** a helpful, artistic young person; can be a birth or a new idea. **R** obstacles, problems, deviation, distraction.

**TEN** love, friendship, happiness, in home life; success. **R** loss of friendship or harmony; strife, conflict.

**NINE** material success; good health; spiritual wellbeing. **R** imperfections, mistakes.

**EIGHT** abandonment, withdrawal; decline of something minor. **R** joy, feasting, celebration; material success.

**SEVEN** too much daydreaming and wishful thinking; little achievement. **R** determination; virtual sucess.

**SIX** memories, the past, vanished things; perhaps change or a desire for it. **R** living in the past; new opportunities.

**FIVE** loss (not total), regret; hollow friendship or marriage. **R** hope, expectations; promise fulfilled; an old friend returns.

**FOUR** discontent, boredom; hesitation despite want of change. **R** new relationships, possibilites, new beginnings.

**THREE** successful resolution; conclusions; healing. **R** excessive physical pleasure.

**TWO** love, a new friendship or relationship. Passion; harmony. **R** false love or friendship; disharmony; divorce.

**ONE** abundance, joy, happiness; spiritual fulfilment. **R** change, instability.

KING OF CUPS   QUEEN OF CUPS   KNIGHT OF CUPS   PAGE OF CUPS

## SWORDS

**KING** a powerful professional man, wise and full of ideas. **R** cruelty; some evil brilliance.

**QUEEN** a widow, sterile and sad, but perceptive and quick-witted. **R** prudish, narrow-minded.

**KNIGHT** an active young man; adjacent cards show outcome. **R** extravagance, indiscretion.

**PAGE** a perceptive young person; spying, agility; good or evil. **R** unspoken danger; illness.

**TEN** ruin, trouble, pain, sadness, though not death. **R** temporary benefit or profit.

**NINE** indecision; failure and desolation; anxiety. **R** doubt and suspicion; imprisonment or confinement.

**EIGHT** crisis, conflict; difficulty in escaping.

**R** past treachery; difficulties.

**SEVEN** plans; uncertainty; potential failure. **R** good advice or instruction.

**SIX** a journey, perhaps by water; success; resolution of difficulties. **R** no solution.

**FIVE** physical conquest, or a threat of defeat and dishonour. **R** uncertaintly, weakness.

**FOUR** respite, recuperation; exile or solitude. **R** activity; economy and care.

**THREE** separation, sorrow, absence, delay. **R** distraction, disorder, confusion.

**TWO** stalemate through balanced forces; harmony; truce. **R** falsehood, release.

**ONE** great force or hatred; excess; fertility. **R** self-destruction from extremes.

## PENTACLES

**KING** an intelligent and successful person, strong character; may be leader. **R** corruption, perversity, dissipation, intoxication.

**QUEEN** prosperity, opulence, security; a rich but generous person. **R** suspicion, neglect, mistrust.

**KNIGHT** a reliable and methodical young man; hard-working and patient. **R** idleness, stagnation, laziness, carelessness.

**PAGE** a careful and diligent young person; scholarship; new idea sought. **R** dissipation and rebellion.

**TEN** a prosperous lineage; gain; family matters; home. **R** loss of money or family reputation.

**NINE** something accomplished; material or financial security; prudence. **R** danger; a threat to safety or possessions.

**EIGHT** an apprenticeship; skill; a future commission. **R** ambition lacking; failure.

**SEVEN** business growth via hard work; success; barter. **R** anxiety and impatience, especially over money.

**SIX** generosity: success shared with others. **R** greed, selfishness, envy.

**FIVE** poverty, loneliness; spiritual or emotional loss. **R** reversal of bad fortune; marriage problems.

**FOUR** obsessed with material wealth; miserly **R** setbacks, obstacles, loss.

**THREE** mastery of a skill in business or art; mobility. **R** lack of skill and care; pettinesss.

**TWO** problems with new projects; agility needed; some harmony. **R** enjoyment simulated; written messages.

**ONE** perfection, bliss, even ecstasy; riches. **R** wealth corrupts; unhappiness.

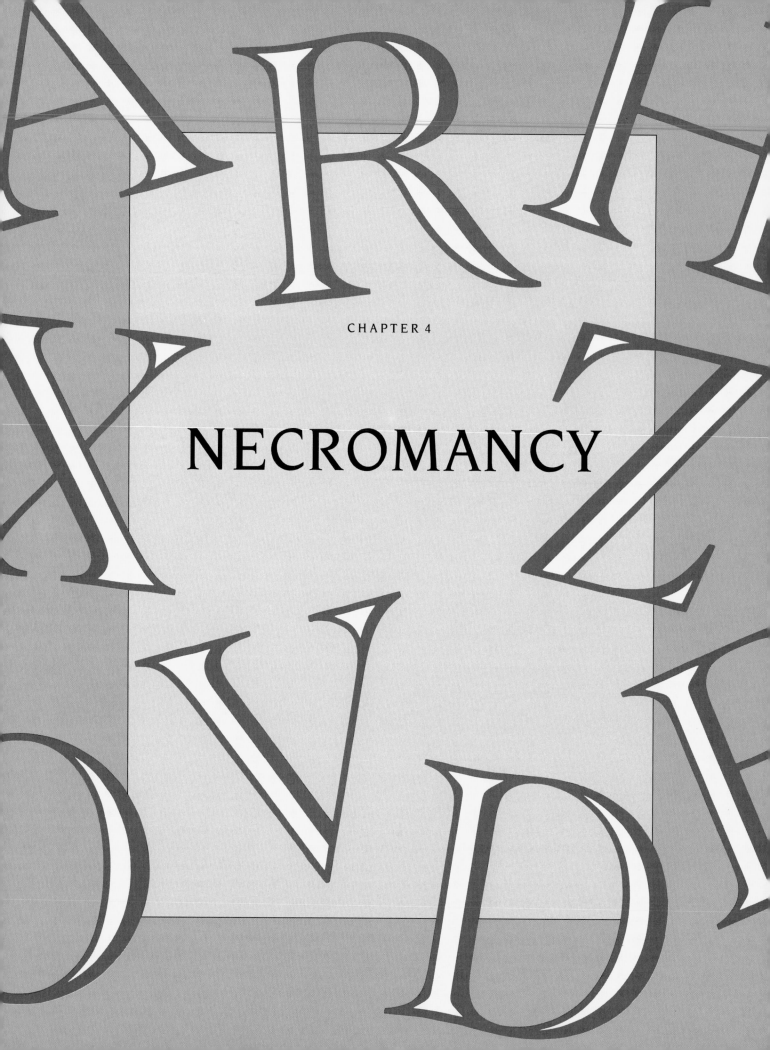

CHAPTER 4

# NECROMANCY

The meaning of necromancy is divination through communication with the dead. Despite the popular conception (created and maintained over the years by scores of horror movies) that it involves bringing the dead back to life, using black magic and producing zombies, necromancy is no more than a form of brief mental contact between our world and the spirit world.

## SPIRITUALISM

Spiritualists communicate with the dead, with those people who are "in spirit", as they put it. This is sometimes at small séances of perhaps half a dozen people, sometimes at services in Spiritualist churches attended by maybe fifty people, and sometimes at large public meetings where hundreds are present. However, spiritualists intentions are not to find out details of the future. They seek only to provide comfort for the living by assuring grieving relatives that their loved ones are happy, content and are still thinking of them.

It is only very occasionally that a medium will receive (from the spirit world) and will pass on (to a member of the audience or congregation) a true prediction. All mediums seem to have had a few such experiences, though. For example, Doris Stokes, the best-known British medium of the last twenty years, always insisted that she did not tell fortunes, yet she mentions a few predictions in *Voices in My Ear* and her other books. These are predictions that came to her unbidden and later proved to be true.

## CLAIRVOYANCE

Clairvoyants are similar to spiritualists in that they sometimes make predictions, doing so without using any physical aids such as cards, a crystal ball or the sight of their client's hand. They do not claim to obtain their information from the dead, but it is possible that they are doing this without knowing it. The meaning of clairvoyance is knowing something that one could not know by normal means (by use of the ordinary senses). There seems to be a touch of clairvoyance in many branches of fortune telling,

53

*A spiritualist (top left in picture) leading a séance.*

something that enables the fortune teller to be more precise than by means of a straightforward interpretation of, for example, dreams or of the tarot would allow. Also, there are many cases on record of people without any psychic ability receiving occasional predictive flashes of knowledge. Could this knowledge perhaps come from the dead?

# PLANCHETTES AND OUIJA BOARDS

Generally, the communication with the dead that produces divinatory messages uses a planchette or a ouija board. There is some similarity between these two and they are often confused with each other.

A planchette is a mobile writing device. It is a small board supported on free-running castors an inch or so above the surface on which it moves – usually a table. Attached is a pencil that just touches the table or, more usefully, touches a large piece of blank paper laid on the table. Several people simultaneously each rest a finger very lightly on the planchette, neither trying to push it nor obstruct it. With luck, the planchette may move across the paper leaving written words in its wake.

Of course, to obtain any useful response from the planchette the conditions must be suitable. The room should be dimly lit, perhaps by candles to create the right atmosphere. The participants need to be genuinely interested in receiving a message from the spirit world, and at least one of them should be sensitive to spirits so that he or she can be used by the spirit to move the planchette. On occasion the planchette can give astonishing results, with the spirits of the dead providing details of the future, but not often.

## ORIGINS OF THE OUIJA BOARD AND MAKING YOUR OWN

While the planchette is claimed to have been known to the ancient Chinese (who greatly revered the spirits of the dead and frequently communicated with them), the ouija board is of much more recent origin. It dates only from the last few years of the nineteenth century and was thought up by an American, William Field. He may have had hopes of contacting foreign-speaking spirits, since he named his invention after the French and German words for "yes".

The planchette and, in particular, the ouija board, have been popular as games, sometimes for young people and even for children. This is

*A planchette being used for spirit writing.*

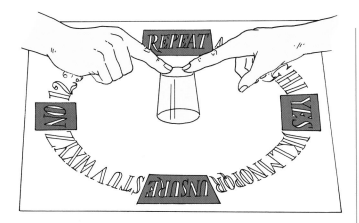

*An ouija board being used with a glass.*

An ouija board is generally made of wood, polished and shiny. It has the letters of the alphabet, the numbers I to 9 and a few useful words such as "Yes", "No", "Repeat", "Hello" and "Goodbye" painted on it. These may be either in a circle around the board or arranged in rows or arcs, somewhat resembling a typewriter keyboard. The moving part may be a planchette on castors, with some kind of pointer. As when using a planchette to write, the fingers of the participants should touch the planchette only lightly. An alternative is to make your own ouija board, utilising any polished wood surface, with the letters, numbers and words written on separate cards and using a drinking glass upside-down to slide from letter to letter. Questions are asked aloud and the answers are spelt out by the movement of the glass.

unfortunate, as neither device is intended to be a game. Any communication with the spirit world is a serious matter which, if undertaken carelessly, may be frightening or lead to considerable emotional trauma, and may be psychically dangerous.

*A group using a planchette on an ouija board to spell out messages.*

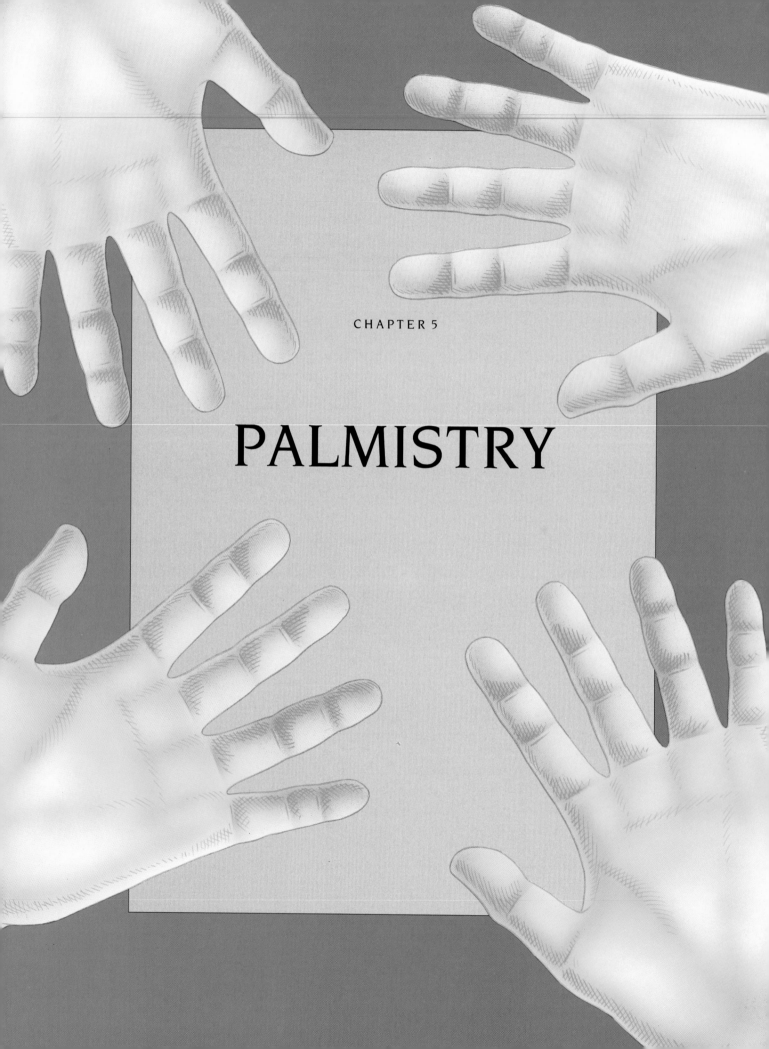

CHAPTER 5

# PALMISTRY

Divination by means of examining the hands (not just the palms, despite the popular name) is of great antiquity. A better name is cheiromancy, from the Greek word *cheir*, meaning hand. It is supposed to have originated in China over 5,000 years ago and to have spread from culture to culture across Asia and the Middle East to Greece, where Aristotle wrote on the subject in about 340 BC. The Romans brought it from Greece to western Europe and it was developed gradually over the centuries by scientists such as Paracelsus (a Swiss physician of the sixteenth century) and Cheiro (Count Louis Hamon, the greatest of the nineteenth century palmists). The claim that it was started by the Gypsies, or even brought to Europe by them, has no basis in fact.

# PALMISTRY TODAY

Today palmistry is still very popular in the West, perhaps because it seems so simple, requiring no equipment. Yet it is deceptively complex, demanding much knowledge and experience if it is to be practised with any accuracy.

Anyone who does practice cheiromancy in a proper manner will not attempt to give a reading without careful consideration of both the subject's hands. The left hand shows the subject's potential from birth while the right hand reveals present character and future events. If the subject is left-handed it is is the other way round. The lines always vary between a pair of hands. They are present from the moment when a baby is born, and they change slightly during the course of the years.

57

*A palmist painted by Pietro della Vecchia in the seventeenth century.*

It is important that you should not expect too much from cheiromancy. It is a form of prophecy that can provide useful suggestions about your health, job prospects, marital harmony (or otherwise) and general success, but it is not usually very precise. Where a more exact reading is given, it is likely that the palmist is using the reading of the hands as merely a starting point and is getting more information by means of some form of clairvoyance, pre-cognition or suchlike.

Some general indications of the subject's personality and capabilities will come from a scrutiny of the shapes of the hands, fingers and fingernails and from their colour and feel.

## HANDSHAPE

● A *practical* hand, with a broad palm and short fingers, indicating a down-to-earth, hard-working, industrious nature.
● An *intuitive* hand, with a long palm and short fingers, indicating a quick, restless person, tending to be an individualist.
● A *sensitive* hand, with a long palm and long fingers, suggesting a person of strong emotions and imagination, and perhaps a volatile or introverted character.
● An *intellectual* hand, with a short palm and long fingers, suggesting an orderly, clear-thinking person, perhaps articulate.

An older classification system recognizes seven hand shapes. It is even claimed that different hand-types mean a suitability for different careers. In addition, the general texture of the skin on the hands is important – coarser or finer reflecting a "coarser" or "finer" personality – together with the consistency of the hands, ranging from hard through firm, rubbery and soft, to flabby.

Several shapes of fingers are recognized, each revealing a particular type of individual. The set of the fingers in relation to the hand (whether one begins lower on the palm than others), the closeness of the fingers and the relative lengths of the different fingers and joints all have their various meanings.

## FINGER NAILS (ONYCHOMANCY)

The finger nails, too, are classified, with the following meanings.

● *Short, broad nails:* critical, quick-tempered, lacking in self-control.
● *Short nails:* enthusiastic, scientific.
● *Long, broad nails:* rational, perhaps with good judgment, timid.
● *Long, oval nails:* easy-going, serene, courteous.
● *Wedge-shaped nails:* very sensitive.
● *Large, squarish nails:* sad, cold, perhaps selfish.

It is worth remembering that, however, well-manicured or neglected – or even chewed – the finger nails are, they will reveal their basic shapes and their owner's characteristics. Reading finger nails is a whole, complex area of divination in itself, known as onychomancy (from *onyx*, the Greek word for a nail).

## THE THUMB

The thumb, of course, has a similarly wide range of shapes. A long thumb suggests powers of leadership, while a very long thumb might be the sign of a tyrannical person. A large thumb denotes a capable, strong-minded, energetic type, and a small thumb suggests one lacking will power and energy. A flexible thumb denotes tolerance and extravagance, while a stiff one indicates reserve, caution, even stubbornness. The thumb's thickness, positioning and the nature and relative lengths of the joints have additional meanings, especially when these factors are taken in combination with all the other features of the hand.

## THE PALM

Both detailed diagrams of the palm and your own hands usually display a bewildering variety of lines and areas. On diagrams these are all carefully named, but on your own hand they are often difficult to identify, or even to find at all. Do not be put off by this. Concentrate on finding the three clearest lines first. They are the Heart Line, the Head Line and the Life Line.

58

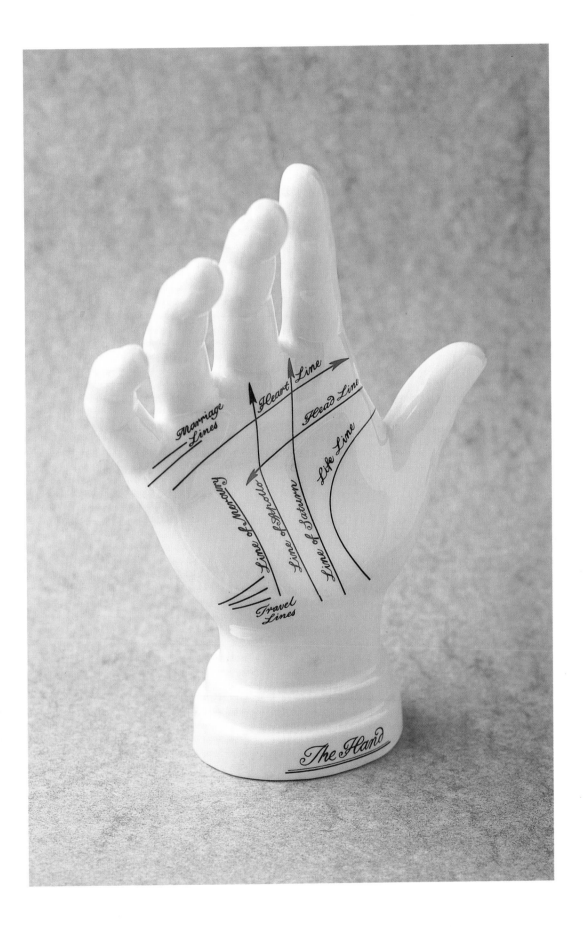

# THE HEART LINE

The Heart Line is the line controlling temperament and emotional health. Its shape and strength are generally taken as signs of the person's capacity for love.

The normal starting point for the Heart Line is on or just below the Mount of Jupiter, at the base of the index finger. From here it may drop down a little before running straight across the hand.

A long, clearly marked line signifies a very steadfast, warm-hearted person. Where the Heart Line is more strongly marked than the Head Line, the Heart Line rules the head (and vice versa).

If the Heart Line begins between the Mounts of Jupiter and Saturn (between the first two fingers) and curves down, the person is said to be very sympathetic and very sensual. A faint Heart Line indicates only limited ability to love, while a Heart Line closer to the fingers suggests a jealous nature. If the line begins only on the Mount of Saturn, the person may still be sensual, but will not really care for other people.

Where the Heart Line begins on the Head Line, the person will be the envious kind. If the Life Line, too, is involved in a three-way beginning, the disposition is probably unreasonable.

Lots of small branches to the Heart Line indicate a flirtatious person. Breaks in the line or a chained line suggest unfaithfulness.

# THE HEAD LINE

In general, the Head Line indicates the depth of understanding, level of intelligence and intellectual ability. The longer the line, the better.

The Head Line usually begins on the Life Line, almost half-way between the thumb and index finger. It goes across the palm either straight towards the Upper Mount of Mars or curving down towards the Mount of Luna.

Where the Head Line goes straight across the palm, the person is practical, a good organizer. If the line slopes towards the Mount of Luna, the person is imaginative with a sensitive nature. If it reaches the mount, it means great imagination. Where the Head Line slopes the other way, towards the Heart Line, good business or financial abilities are suggested, although if it runs along close to the Heart Line, it means a narrow outlook.

If the line is clear and deep for its whole length, the subject will have great powers of concentration, and the subject will be able to commit himself or herself unswervingly to a task. However, any "chaining" or breaks will diminish this power.

Ideally, the Head Line should end in a three-pronged fork, indicating business ability, imagination and intelligence.

# THE LIFE LINE

Not only longevity but also health and vitality can be foretold from this, probably the best known of all lines on the palm.

The longer and clearer it is, the longer and healthier your life will be. Normally the Life Line starts from the Head Line, about half way between the thumb and index finger, indicating a controlled personality. If it begins with a netted effect it suggests a cautious person.

Branches from the Life Line to the Head Line are significant. A forked beginning suggest an ability to understand and help others. A pair of branches up to the Head Line from close to the beginning denotes an inheritance or a good start in life. A branch half-way down indicates success in middle age. Where the Life Line reaches right to the wrist, life will be long, probably until well over seventy years of age.

A tasselled or shallow line suggests lack of vitality, though not necessarily a short life. Breaks in the line are indicative of changes in lifestyle or problems with health.

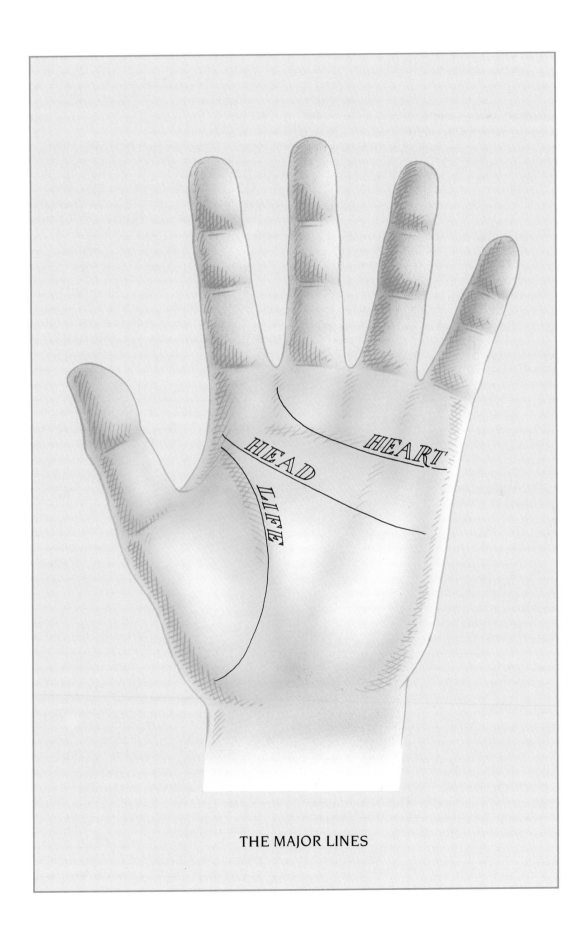

**THE MAJOR LINES**

## THE MOUNTS

Before you try to identify the other lines, which are all less clearly marked, it will help you to learn the names of the various areas of the palm. These are known as mounts, despite the fact that in many people they are hardly any higher than the areas around them and in some cases they are even hollows.

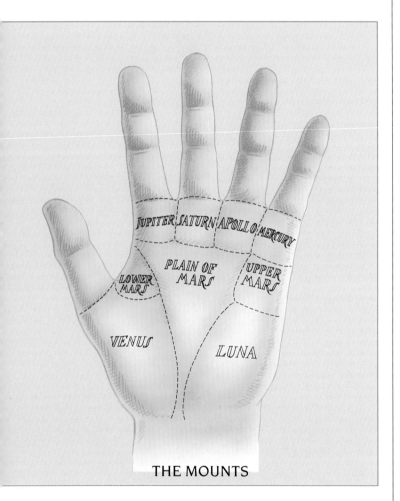

### THE MOUNTS

The great importance of the mounts is that whichever of them is most highly developed on your hands gives its qualities most strongly to your personality and to your health.

If you bend your hand right back at the wrist and hold it up at eye level you will be able to see more easily which of your mounts is most highly developed. Often two or three mounts are equally developed, giving a well-balanced character that is made up of the qualities of both or all three. Occasionally all the mounts seem to be about equal, in which case the personality will be equable and life will most likely be smooth and happy.

Because all the mounts have their good and bad aspects, the markings on the most prominent mount or mounts must be studied carefully. The general rule is that vertical lines are good signs and horizontal lines are bad signs, although a hatching of vertical and horizontal lines to form a grille is a bad sign, while a star is a good sign.

Here are some of the main characteristics of people who have a particular one of the mounts predominating.

**The Mount of Jupiter** An ambitious honourable person, perhaps a leader, likely to marry young, liable to digestive troubles resulting from a love of good food; a cross on the mount indicates a happy marriage.

**The Mount of Saturn** A tall, thin, gloomy person, relatively unsociable; a good student, and possibly very musical; perhaps will remain unmarried; may suffer from illnesses such as rheumatism and nervous complaints.

**The Mount of Apollo** Happy, healthy, athletic and very appreciative of art; will marry, but not happily; may suffer from heart trouble.

**The Mount of Mercury** Most easily led into illegalities, especially if the mount shows a grille; otherwise good in business and at games; generally healthy except for a tendency to suffer minor stomach problems.

**The Mount of Mars** A complex type because of the upper and lower sections of the mount and the Plain of Mars between. This person will be a fighter, mainly aggressive if the lower section predominates and resistive if the upper does; if the plain is well developed, the subject will be short-tempered; this is a stubborn, persistent individual, healthy and energetic.

**The Mount of Luna** An expressive person of great imagination, but a dreamer, tending towards the impractical; of weak health.

**The Mount of Venus** A loving, considerate and generous individual, happy though not good in business (as tends to be too honest); may be passionate and often tempted by attraction to the opposite sex; tends to marry young and to be very healthy.

## THE MINOR LINES

### THE LINE OF FATE

Of the minor lines on the palm, the most important is the Line of Fate (or Line of Saturn), which is normally (but by no means always) present for part of the way between the wrist and the Mount of Saturn. It is the career line, indicating how successful and how settled you are and will be in your chosen career. If it begins on the Mount of Luna this suggests success in your profession – but with considerable help from a member of the opposite sex. If it begins in the middle of the palm and runs all the way to the Mount of Saturn it indicates success through your own efforts. Where the line begins further up the hand, this means an uneventful, perhaps idle or unsuccessful early life.

A sharply defined Line of Fate is most propitious. Where it is thin it means you need to work very hard for success; where it is chained it suggests difficulties. If the line is absent altogether (or only very shallow) you may still be able to overcome this handicap and achieve some success. A bar cutting across the Line of Fate denotes a serious obstacle, and a break in the line means a complete change. If the line continues after a break, look carefully to see whether it does so a little closer to the thumb (indicating an improvement in your general career situation) or away from it (the opposite).

Sometimes the Line of Fate does not end on the Mount of Saturn but runs across (perhaps via a branch) to the Mount of Jupiter, indicating a great success through ambition, or to the Mount of Apollo, indicating some artistic success. If the line ends short of the Mount of Saturn it may mean an early end to your career or merely an eventful later career.

### THE LINE OF APOLLO

The Line of Apollo (or Success) is not found on all hands. Where it does exist it ends on or close to the Mount of Apollo, although its beginning may be on the Mount of Luna, the Plain of Mars or the Life Line. It is, generally, a sign of the prospect of accomplishment, and the longer the line the more will be accomplished. As with the Line of Fate, it can be age-linked, with its presence closer to the Mount of Apollo indicating success in later life. Also, if the line is absent, wavy or chained, you can expect little success, and breaks or bars indicate there will be set-backs or barriers to success.

### THE LINE OF MERCURY

The Line of Mercury (or Health) runs towards the Mount of Mercury, sometimes from the wrist end

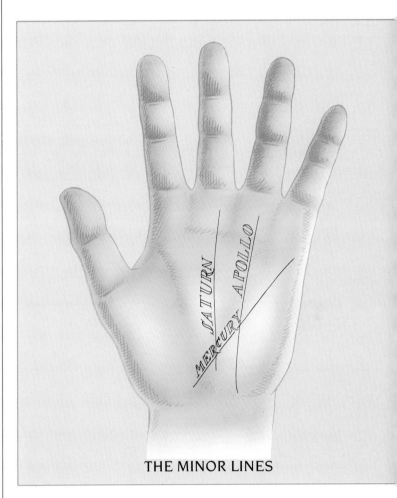

## THE MINOR LINES

of the Mount of Luna. While a clear, deep line suggests a life free from illness so, ironically, does an absence of the line. A chained line predicts liver troubles, a broad, shallow line indicates stomach problems, while dots, bars and breaks on the line suggest illness to come at those age points. An island on the line is the worst of all signs, indicating suffering to come.

Many other minor lines exist, at least on some people's palms, so, if you have a real interest, you should consult a book on the subject.

CHAPTER 6

# NUMEROLOGY

Numbers control all our lives. It is very simple to calculate which particular number or numbers represent you and then to look up the prophecies associated with those numbers. Numerology (or arithromancy, as it is sometimes known) is easily mastered, requiring no great amount of knowledge, no apparatus and no skill. It is an ancient form of divination, but it has connections with astrology and, as with the tarot, its origins have been lost in the mists of time.

The only complexity (or uncertainty) about numerology is that there are many slightly different systems to which this chapter is only a brief introduction. In most cases you need to calculate a single-digit number that represents you. Most important is your birth number, because this should reflect your innate characteristics. Also of significance, because it reflects your development through life, is your name number.

## FINDING YOUR BIRTH NUMBER

To find your birth number, first add up the day, month and year figures of your date of birth. For example, if your date of birth is June 15, 1966, you need to add 6 (June is the sixth month) + 1+5 (the days as separate figures) + 1 + 9 + 6 + 6 (the year) which gives 34. To arrive at a single number, simply add the two digits 3 + 4, giving 7. This is the birth number.

An alternative approach, equally simple, was suggested by Cheiro, the famous late-nineteenth-century palmist and numerologist. Here the year and month are ignored, so that the birth number is determined by your day of birth alone. A person born on the first day of the month has the birth number of 1. But so also does the person born on the 10th, 19th or 28th (add the digits together, ignoring zeroes). Under this system, the person born on June 15th 1966 has a birth number of 6 (+5) as does anybody born on the 15th of any month of any year.

## FINDING YOUR NAME NUMBER

If you want to find your name number, write down the most commonly used form of your name (not necessarily your full name) and convert the letters using the table below.

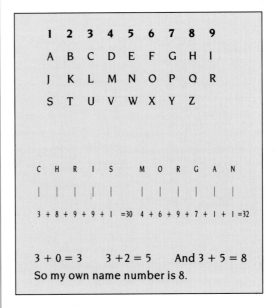

But once again there is another approach. An older system of number-letter equivalents (supposedly of very great antiquity) leaves out the number 9. This is because the number 9 represents the 9-letter name of God and must not be used. It is an old Hebrew taboo. (In the Jewish faith, even the spelling out of the name of God is taboo and is written rather as "G-d".

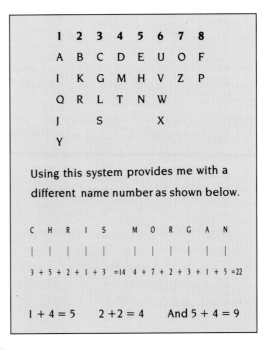

# MEANINGS OF NUMBERS

## 1

One represents the beginning, the One (in the sense of a creator) and also the Sun. People with this number have great leadership qualities, sometimes with enough success, dominance and aggression to be ruthless. So it is a powerful number. Use your power carefully and others will look up to you. Use it carelessly and you may be guilty of being self-centred and tyrannical. This number equates with the tarot card The Magician. Your best days (of any month) are the 1st, 10th, 19th and 28th, especially when one of them falls on a Sunday (although Monday is almost as lucky for you). Your best colours are brown and yellow and your lucky stones are topaz and amber.

## 2

The Moon is associated with number two. It is a "feminine" number, gentle and intuitive, more concerned with thought than action. Compatibility is great with one people. Twos are inventive and articulate. Beware of indecisiveness, a lack of self-confidence and deceit. Your best days are the 2nd, 11th, 20th or 29th and any Monday. Your colours are green, cream and white and your stones are jade, pearl and moonstone. Your tarot card is The High Priestess.

## 3

Three is a creative number, its people tending to be disciplined and successful. Jupiter is the guiding planet. The best days of the month are the 3rd, 12th, 21st or 30th, with Thursdays particularly good. Your relationships will be especially fruitful with other threes. Beware of a tendency towards bossiness. Your colours are in the mauve, violet and purple range. Your stone is amethyst. Your tarot card is The Empress.

## 4

Because four is a square and thus a complete number, representing the seasons, people born under its influence may be square (in the sense of dull), earthbound and unimaginative. These are also people who seem to delight in being rebellious, taking an opposite view to everyone else. Making friends is difficult so, if this applies to you, you must beware of feeling too lonely and isolated. Your lucky days are the 4th, 13th, 22nd and 31st, you are represented by the planet Uranus, and Sunday is your best day. Bright blue and grey are your colours and sapphire is your stone. Your tarot card is The Emperor.

## 5

Symbolised by Mercury, five is the number of the senses. Its people are mercurial – impulsive, unpredictable, active, eloquent and ever-changing. Sensual pleasure is important here (from the five senses). Number five people have the knack of making friends easily with anybody (especially with other fives). Your greatest flaws are being highly strung and hating routine or restrictions. Your lucky days are the 5th, 14th and 22nd and Wednesdays. Most lighter colours suit you and your stone is diamond. Your tarot card is The Hierophant.

# 6

The emotions are important with six, because of the influence of Venus. The love represented is more romantic or family love than sexual. It is a "perfect" number because it is the sum of its factors (1, 2 and 3). Number six people tend to be reliable, domestic and fond of beauty. If you are a six you know that you can also be obstinate. But even so, you will be very popular, making many friends. You have many lucky days: the 3rd, 6th, 9th, 12th, 15th, 18th, 21st, 27th and 30th, as well as any Friday. You can wear any shade of blue or pink. Your lucky stones are turquoise and emerald and your tarot card is The Lovers.

# 7

Most significant of all the numbers, seven is generally thought of as lucky because there have been so many famous groups of seven or of its multiples: the days of the week, phases of the Moon, notes of the musical scale, colours of the spectrum, the seven original fixed stars, the seven graces, the seven virtues and, from the Bible, seven days of creation, seven trumpets, seven plagues, seven seas and many more. Its great mysticism is summed up in the belief that a seventh son of a seventh son will possess enormous magical powers. So the number is regarded as highly spiritual and philosophical. Its people are intuitive, perhaps psychic, and not interested in material wealth. If you are a seven person, you have great associations with water, your planet being Neptune, so you will tend to love travel, especially on the sea. You often have power over others, but must avoid being too introverted. Your originality can make you a good writer, poet or painter. The 7th, 16th and 25th are your lucky days, together with any Monday. Your best colour is green and your stone is moss-agate. The associated tarot card is The Chariot.

# 8

Eight is a strange and contradictory number in which there are echoes of the rebelliousness of four. Governed by Saturn, number-eight people must suffer sorrow along with any success. If you are an eight person, you possess great will power and individuality, yet you are always misunderstood, partly as a result of hiding your strong feelings beneath a cold exterior. You must try to be more open, less intense, and strive to make friends. Your best days are Saturdays and the 8th, 17th and 26th days of the month. Dark colours suit you best, in the range of dark grey, black, dark blue and purple. Your stone is amethyst, a dark sapphire or even a black pearl. Your tarot card is Strength, and strength is what you need to triumph over such an unlucky number as eight.

# 9

A number as sacred as seven, nine is numerologically the ultimate because when multiplied by any other number it reproduces itself (eg $3 \times 9 = 27$, then $2 + 7 = 9$). It has Biblical connections (a trinity of trinities and the nine orders of angels, for example), represents the nine months of pregnancy, the nine spheres of ancient cosmology and the nine lives of a cat. Nines are active, determined, fighters (the influence of their planet Mars), accident-prone, quarrelsome and impulsive. They get on well with threes and sixes. If you are nine, your lucky days are the 3rd, 6th, 9th, 12th, 15th, 18th, 21st, 24th, 27th and 30th, and Tuesdays. Your colours are ruby, garnet and bloodstone. Your tarot card is The Hermit.

# US PRESIDENTS DYING IN OFFICE

*John F. Kennedy*

68

There is a very strange numerological sequence concerning Presidents of the United States. Every twenty years, from 1840 to 1960 the president elected that year died before completing his term of office.

William H. Harrison – elected in 1840

Abraham Lincoln – elected in 1860

James A. Garfield – elected in 1880

William McKinley – elected in 1900

Warren G. Harding – elected in 1920

Franklin D. Roosevelt – elected in 1940

John F. Kennedy – elected in 1960

It has been suggested that Harrison was the victim of an Amerindian curse, from the Shawnee chief, Tecumseh, which continued down the years. After a run of seven such tragedies (a magical number, which might well have been the limit of such a curse), President Ronald Reagan, who was elected in 1980, completed his term of office. Reagan was, however, hit by an assassin's bullet and was within an inch or two of being the eighth in the sequence.

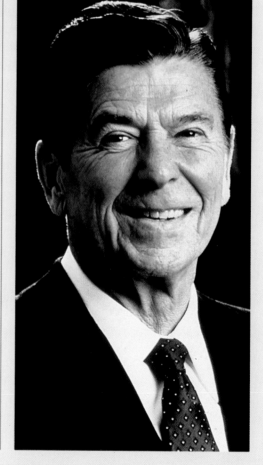

*Ronald Reagan*

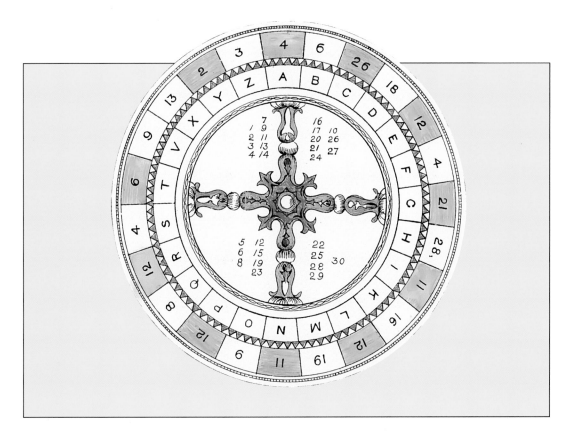

*A numerological "wheel of fortune", originating from the seventeenth century.*

69

## NUMBERS OVER NINE

What the numerologists call "secondary numbers", those over 9, are also sometimes used in determining fortunes. Up to 52 (the weeks in a year) they all possess meanings, and up to 22 they have strong connections with the tarot pack's Major Arcana, which also bear those numbers. For example, 11, 12 and 13 (Justice, The Hanged Man and Death, respectively) are held to be unlucky numbers, while 17 (The Star), 19 (The Sun) and 21 (The World) are fortunate, boding well for future events.

Why should numbers over 9 be significant at all, when they can all be reduced so easily to single digits? The answer is that sometimes these secondary numbers are obviously important in a person's life, with the same number recurring. For example, suppose that you were born on the 12th day of the month (or, especially, on the 12th of December), that you are constantly ranked 12th in exams, that you marry on the 12th, live at house number 12, divorce after 12 years and so on. It would seem folly to ignore such a number and abbreviate it (1 + 2) to 3. Such a number, influential or fateful, is known as a "fadic" number (perhaps from *fado*, the Portuguese word for fate).

## NUMBER THIRTEEN

The number 13 is almost always considered unlucky. In American in particular, some buildings do not have a storey numbered 13, and some hotels have no room 13. In Italian theatres there are often no seats numbered 13.

This belief that 13 is an unlucky number may originate from the tarot pack, where number 13 of the Major Arcana is Death. Alternatively, there may be a connection with Judas Iscariot, the thirteenth man at the Last Supper. Although 13 is the traditional number of witches in a coven, whether it has been deliverately chosen by witches to parody the Last Supper is unclear. A "Baker's dozen" of 13 loaves is supposed by one theory to mean the Devil's dozen, from Boucca (an old English name for a spirit).

In fact there seems to be no truth in the idea of "unlucky 13". For some people it is a fadic number of great good fortune. Certainly it has never been unlucky in Far Eastern cultures, and the formation of the original 13 states of the American Union has not proved unlucky. A good example of the number 13 being lucky was James Buchanan (13 letters), a Pennsylvanian (13 letters), who was the 13th President of the United States.

# CRYSTALLOMANCY

*Crystal balls are usually made of glass and spherical.*

Crystallamonacy, or divination by looking into a crystal ball, is the only variation of scrying commonly used today. Scrying (simply an old English word for seeing) was practised by many early civilizations. Originally, a clear, still pool of water was used for the purpose, and one can still look into a bowl or bucket of water, or a pool of ink for predictive shapes, although this is not much done these days. A mirror, either of clear or dark glass, can also be used – this form of divination is known as catoptromancy. Even a polished surface of metal or stone may be used for scrying.

The important point about all these methods is that there must be a reflective surface upon which the scryer can fix his or her attention.

## CRYSTAL BALLS

Crystal balls have increased in popularity in the West over recent years. Rock Crystal was originally used. Beryl is better for the purpose, and even more expensive. Most crystal balls today are made of clear glass; even so, they can cost a great deal of money.

It is far better (for psychic reasons) to be given a crystal rather than to buy one yourself. If you must buy one, it is best to avoid mail order.

Always handle the crystal before purchasing it to make sure that it feels right to you. A size of about 4in/10 cm in diameter is best, but the size and shape must suit you personally. Most crystals sold today are spherical, though some have a flat side ground into them so that they can be free-standing without a support; there are others which are oval. The shape is a matter of personal preference.

## PREPARING YOUR CRYSTAL

Once you have your crystal, you must prepare it for use. Different scryers offer different advice for this, although most recomend a careful wash. Running water is best, especially from a natural source like a stream. Rain water collected and poured over it will probably suffice. Then rinse the crystal with vinegar and polish it with velvet or chamois leather. The crystal must always be kept clean and out of bright or direct light. Keep it carefully wrapped in a piece of black velvet or black silk when you are not using it.

Some scryers say that the crystal needs to be charged up with psychic energy, either just when it is new or each time before use. This charging may be done simply by the scryer holding the crystal in his or her hands and consciously willing it to be energized by the spirit world.

## SETTING THE SCENE

There is little agreement among scryers as to the best conditions for crystallomancy. Quietness is generally preferred, although some scryers are willing and able to operate in the noise and bustle of a psychic fair, surrounded by other fortune-tellers and their clients. Dim light is also preferred, so that there are not reflections to interfere with images seen in the crystal, but a few scryers can function well in bright conditions, and a few prefer complete darkness. Twilight is usually regarded as the most propitious time for scrying.

Whether or not your subject (questioner) should be given the crystal to handle for a few moments before the scrying is a matter of sharply-divided opinion; there are some scryers who always give the crystal to their subject, whereas others feel that it would ruin a crystal if anybody else touched it (the subject may, however, be asked to put his or her hands close to it). In any case, the subject should be present and be thinking about a problem or question. The scryer must be in a tranquil and receptive state of mind. For a few minutes the scryer will see nothing, and then images will begin to appear in the crystal.

## WHAT THE "CLOUDS" SAY

For most scryers the crystal becomes misty first, and as the mist clears, the true visions of the future can be seen. These true visions are often no more than cloudy masses of no distinct shape. Here the colour is important.

White is the best, signifying good luck. Green clouds mean there is hope. Blue clouds, too, are a good sign. Yellow means jealousy. Red and orange clouds are signs of danger, perhaps of hatred. Worst of all is black, which portends evil.

When a question is being asked by the subject, the clouds can supply an answer by their direction, with rising clouds meaning "yes" and descending clouds meaning "no".

Some scryers can distinguish not just clouds but shapes and even scenes from the future. The shapes are most often symbolic, with fairly obvious meanings – a skull suggesting death and so on. It is further claimed that the position of the shape or picture in the crystal can indicate time, with future events right at the front and past events at the back.

If you are trying to tell fortunes from a crystal and are seeing nothing, do not despair. It takes a good deal of practice and concentration. You must persevere.

72

*A scryer concentrates hard as she gazes into the crystal.*

## NOSTRADAMUS 1503-66

The real name of Nostradamus was Michel de Notre Dame, who was French and compiled probably the most famous set of prophecies ever made. Although the prophecies themselves are well known because several books about them have been published in recent years, it is not generally realised that he seems to have obtained most of his visions of the future by scrying.

As with most early fortune-tellers, Nostradamus's methods of operation are not exactly known. What is known is that sometimes he used a "magic" mirror. This is variously described as a large glass mirror supported upright on a mantlepiece, and as a disc of brightly polished steel lying on a table. He is also supposed to have made considerable use of a brass bowl filled with water. It is probable that he managed to "see" his prophecies in any shiny surface.

He was very successful, both in his own time as an advisor to Henry II and Catherine de Medici of France, and later because of his prophecies concerning events from the sixteenth century through to the twentieth century. These prophecies include, notably, what seem to be references to Napoleon and Hitler.

# CHAPTER 8

# PLAYING CARDS

Cartomancy is the word for telling fortunes with ordinary playing cards. It is a form of divination that has been around for almost as long as the cards themselves, from the early Middle Ages. Over the years many different predictive meanings have been given to the individual cards and to the combination in which they appear. Some card readers recognize changed meanings for reversed cards (as in tarot readings) while others do not. A further complication is that most readers seem to employ their own, quite various methods as to the number of cards used and the manner and order of laying them out.

Consequently, this chapter can give only some indications of a very diverse and varying method of fortune telling.

## THE PACK AND THE SUITS

The standard British and American pack of playing cards consists of 52 cards arranged into four suits. The suits are hearts, clubs, diamonds and spades. Each suit contains the numbered cards one (Ace) to ten and the court cards – a Jack, a Queen and a King. This is different from the tarot pack and different also from the packs in common use in continental Europe.

## PSYCHIC ELEMENTS

Later on, this chapter will explain some methods of laying out the cards and something about interpreting them for fortunes. But you must not think of this as a mechanical procedure that anyone can perform. In order to read the future in cards, you need to be sensitive to the overall meaning of the cards that turn up and at the same time, be sensitive to the person whose fortune you are trying to read. There are psychic elements to cartomancy in the way that there are to many other methods of divination.

## GENERAL TIPS

You can improve your chances of giving accurate reading in several ways. One is to buy a new pack of cards and reserve them for fortunes. If you wish to consider the more negative meanings of reversed cards, you will need to do something such as mark one end of the pack with a pencil. Do not let other people handle your cards except for the questioner at the start of a reading (who should be allowed to cut them, at least). Make sure that the conditions suit you – the correct light level and no distractions. Take your time shuffling the cards. Never rush through a reading. Use a prompt sheet of interpretations if you need to, but let your inner feelings guide you. You are advised not to read your own fortunes in the cards, nor indeed to perform a reading for somebody who is not present.

You can either deal cards from the whole 52-card pack for your reading or else you can reduce it to a 32-card pack. This is done by discarding the twos, threes, fours, fives and sixes of each suit. The 32-card is more commonly used by professional card readers.

## COMPARING CARD-PACKS

| Type of pack | No. of cards | Suits | Court cards |
| --- | --- | --- | --- |
| **UK & US** | 52 | Hearts, Clubs, Diamonds, Spades | Jack, Queen, King |
| **Tarot** | 78 | Cups, Staves/Batons, Coins/Pentacles, Swords | Page, Knight, Queen, King |
| **French** | 52 | Hearts, Trefoils, Tiles, Spades/Pikeheads | Valet, Queen, King |
| **German** | 36 | Shields, Leaves/Flowers, Hawk bells, Acorns | Unter, Ober, König |
| **Spanish** | 52 | Cups, Staves, Coins, Swords | Jack, Queen/Knight, King |
| **Italian** | 40 | Cups, Staves, Coins, Swords | Page, Knight, King |

## THE CARD MEANINGS

Particular combinations are ignored here, and the meanings are given for the 32-card pack only. **R** means the card is reversed.

### HEARTS

ACE      romantic love, friendship, a happy home-life. **R** unsettled at home.

KING      a good-natured, fair-haired man, offering sound professional advice. **R** an unreliable person.

QUEEN    a fair-haired woman, faithful and affectionate. **R** a spiteful person.

JACK      a friend, a happy young person. **R** short-tempered.

TEN      an excellent card; ambitions achieved; joy, love, luck. **R** short-term problems.

NINE      wishes fulfilled; good health; improvements all round. **R** temporary setbacks.

EIGHT    invitations, visits, pleasurable journeys, perhaps romance. **R** unrequited love.

SEVEN    wisdom, imagination, self-sufficiency. **R** boredom.

### CLUBS

ACE      happiness, wealth and good health. **R** short-lived happiness.

KING      a dark haired man, honest and generous. **R** small troubles.

QUEEN    a dark-haired woman, romantic and capable. **R** initiative, craftiness.

JACK      a reliable friend, skilful and enterprising. **R** an insincere lover.

TEN      unexpected money coming. **R** a journey, minor problems.

NINE      immediate achievement, sudden opportunity. **R** disappointing receipts.

EIGHT    a gamble; choose your partner carefully, **R** unhappy in love.

SEVEN    small benefits; goodwill from repayments. **R** small money problems.

### DIAMONDS

ACE      a letter or a ring; important. **R** bad news.

KING      an obstinate man, powerful, fair-haired. **R** deception penetrated.

QUEEN    a flirtatious fair-haired woman. **R** a spiteful gossip.

JACK      an official (perhaps a relation); unreliable. **R** a troublemaker.

TEN      changes involving money, a journey, jobs. **R** similiar, but with problems.

NINE      surprise; beware of self-interest. **R** domestic disputes.

EIGHT    pleasant journeys; a late marriage. **R** beware of hasty romance.

SEVEN    social chat; news. **R** tiny problems magnified.

### SPADES

ACE      love affairs, perhaps unhappy; caution needed. **R** bad news, bad luck, death.

KING      an ambitious dark-haired man, a bad enemy. **R** an unscrupulous enemy.

QUEEN    a dark-haired widow, unscrupulous. **R** a crafty and spiteful person.

JACK      a rough diamond, well-meaning. **R** an untrustworthy person.

TEN      worry, unhappiness, emotional distress. **R** illness, loss.

NINE      all-round bad luck; conflict and loss. **R** unhappiness, misfortunes.

EIGHT    trouble approaching; illness and anxiety. **R** sorrow in relationships.

SEVEN    worries, perhaps imagined. **R** bad advice, indecision.

77

*Spanish (top row), German (centre row) and Italian (bottom row) playing cards.*

## SPREADING THE CARDS

Note that the details of particular spreads are not fixed by any laws; different readers use slight variations.

As with the significator in tarot readings, a client card may be selected to represent the client or questioner. If it is a fair- or red-haired younger man or woman use the King or Queen of Hearts respectively. For a fair- or grey- or red-haired older man or woman it should be the King or Queen of Diamonds. If a darker-haired younger man or woman, the King or Queen of Clubs. For a darker-haired older person, use the King or Queen of Spades.

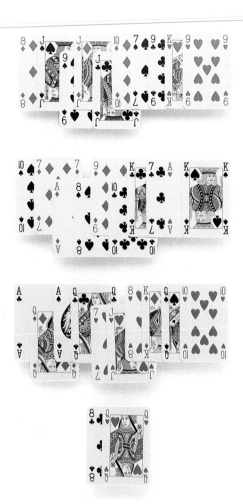

## THE FAN

After shuffling the 32-card pack, lay it face down on the table, well spread out. Then invite the questioner to choose 18 cards. Lay these out face up in the order shown. (see picture). It is important that the client card or significator should be among the first 13 laid out. If not, the seven of the same suit will do. If neither is present, try another spread, or abandon the reading until another time.

Look at cards 1 to 13. Find the client card and, counting that as the first of a group of five cards (moving to the right), give a reading of the fifth card. This card then becomes the first of a new group of five as you move to the right again. Continue to interpret the fifth card each time until, eventually, your fifth card is the client card (which you must also interpret). Then move to the five cards laid out beneath the others. Interpret the end one (cards 14 and 18) together, then cards 15 and 17 together, and finally card 16. This should provide a fairly good general forecast of the questioner's life.

## A SIMPLE CARD-READING SYSTEM

If you lack expertise in card-reading, try this simple system first. Shuffle a 32-card pack carefully, especially end-to-end, to produce plenty of reversed cards. Then remove the top and bottom cards and lay them aside, face down, as a surprise for later.

Cut the 30 cards and deal them face down into three equal piles. Turn up the top pile and spread them into an overlapping row so each each card is visible. Look for any reversed cards and push them a little way down, out of line, for easier recognition. This row represents the questioner's past.

Now do the same with the middle and bottom rows, which represent the questioner's present and future respectively. The three rows may be read (taking note of reverses). Finally, retrieve the two surprise cards and turn them over. They may add a different slant to the whole reading.

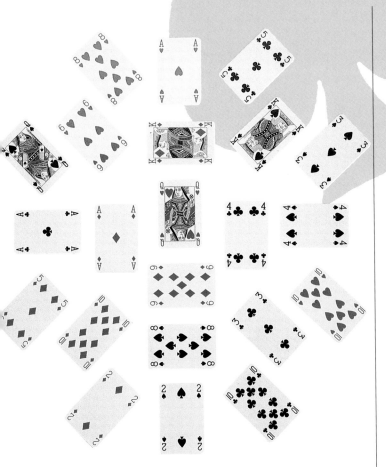

## DO WALSH'S SYSTEM

Here is an example of a personal method of divination practised by a card-reader known to the author. It is simple and may or may not be unique to her. A 32-card pack is used. The questioner or client asks a question (aloud or silently) while shuffling the cards and cutting three times. The reader deals the top 12 cards into three equal piles. It is the centre pile which is the most important, and is turned over and interpreted first. Either the top card is turned over and read on its own, or else the four cards in the pile are turned and read together, depending on the reader's instinct.

If necessary the left-hand pile is interpreted next, then the right-hand pile. In this system, combinations of cards are regarded as being very significant.

Clearly, much more must be put into this reading than just the standard meanings of the cards, which is the way it should always be with divination from playing cards.

79

## THE GRAND STAR

This is a more detailed spread of 21 cards, popular, useful and of long standing. It may also be done from the full 52-card pack, when it is known as the Wheel of Fortune (as above).

Place the significator face up in the middle of the table and then layout the first 21 cards of the shuffled pack *face down* in the order shown. Now begin the reading, interpreting cards in pairs. In addition to their specific meanings, the cards above the significator should be taken as representing the questioner's future accomplishments, while those below it refer to past successes; to the left are potential obstacles, and to the right is a source of help.

The 21 cards must be turned over and read in this order: 13 and 15, 20 and 18, 19 and 17, 9 and 5, 11 and 8, 10 and 6, 12 and 7, 3 and 1, 4 and 2, then card 21 on its own.

CHAPTER NINE

# DREAMS

e all dream, every night, although most of the time we do not remember doing so. Some of these dreams are predictions of future events. Even if we can recall our dreams, it is difficult to decide which ones are predictive and even more difficult to cut through the mass of symbolism to determine their true meanings successfully.

> Dreams are true while they last, and do we not live in dreams? *Alfred. Lord Tennyson.*
> Learn from your dreams what you lack. *W. H. Auden.*
> I had a sort of dream-trance the other day, in which I saw my favourite trees step out and promenade up, down and around, very curious – with a whisper from one, leaning down as he pass'd me. 'We do all this on the present occasion, exceptionally, just for you'. *Walt Whitman.*
> Existence would be intolerable if we were never to dream. *Anatole France.*

## DIFFERENT KINDS OF SLEEP

Research has shown that there are two different kinds of sleep. One is identified by twitches of muscles in the face and body, by slightly irregular breathing, by an increase in blood pressure and by movements of the eyeballs beneath the eyelids. Because of this last characteristic it is known as REM or rapid-eye-movement sleep. The other type of sleep is quieter, with few body movements, regular breathing and no rapid eye movements. It is called NREM or non-rapid-eye-movement sleep. Every night we alternate between these two types of sleep, experiencing about ninety minutes of each, though REM-sleep periods become slightly longer and NREM-period shorter towards morning. If people are woken from REM sleep they nearly always report that they were dreaming; if woken from NREM sleep they hardly ever do.

So we know that REM sleep is associated with dreams and that people generally dream for about half their sleeping time. Furthermore, it has even been suggested that dreaming is a more vital activity than sleep itself. Perhaps we only sleep in order to dream.

## DREAMS AND DIVINATION THROUGH THE AGES

Dreaming has always been regarded as a strange, mystical activity. Using the odd, half-remembered scenes of happenings of our dreams to help predict the future is a very ancient form of divination which is known and used all over the world. It is called oneiromancy, from *oneiros*, the Greek word for a dream.

Some of the earliest written records in existence, from Mesopotamia and ancient Egypt, are concerned with dreams and their interpretation. There was a strong and widely held belief in the ancient world that dreams foretold the future.

The Bible dscribes many dreams that contained detailed instructions or symbolic messages. The most famous is Jacob's dream of a ladder set up between Earth and Heaven. *Genesis* 28: 12-16;. Ancient Greek and Roman literature is full of references to dreams. One early work on the subject has survived, *Oneirocritica* by Artemidorous of Daldi, a Greek who flourished in about AD 140. He believed that the main function of dreams was to enable us to discover the truth by way of symbolic images. "Dreams and visions are infused into men for their advantage and instruction", he wrote. His book is a collection of dream interpretations, which remained the major work on its subject until the nineteenth century.

*An 1843 woodcut of a scene from the Bible, in which Joseph interprets a dream of the Pharaoh.*

### SIGMUND FREUD (1856-1939)

It was towards the end of the nineteenth century that the whole business of interpreting dreams was turned upside-down by developments in the science of psychology. The first great figure was Sigmund Freud, the originator of psychoanalysis, who came to believe – during his studies of the unconscious mind – that dreams are always the wish-fulfilment fantasies of the unconscious mind presented in symbolic form. He maintained that most dreams are sparked off by sexual repressions, so that most dream objects have sexual connotations. To Freud, a snake, a tower or a rifle was a phallic symbol, while a cup, a tunnel or a sack represented a vagina, and the act of dancing, flying or merely turning a key in a lock to open a door represented the sex act itself.

## CARL GUSTAV JUNG (1875-1961)

Jung was a psychologist who disagreed with Freud's theories about dreams, believing instead that there is no general theory to explain all dreams, whether as sexual symbols or anything else. He maintained that interpretations had to be much more fluid, taking into account the personality of the individual. On the whole, he believed that dreams are an attempt by our unconscious to compensate. This is why our dreams are often opposite to the way we normally are, with a hard man being sentimental in his dreams, a timid person showing a fighting spirit, and so on. Not that this rules out predictive dreams, because Jung also recognized what he termed "prospective" dreams (the anticipation of probability) and "telephathic" dreams where a message is received subconsciously (say from a relative or a friend) so that it might seem to predict what we are later told.

## SOME HISTORICAL PREDICTIVE DREAMS

There have been many important predictive dreams recorded over the centuries, which have influenced the lives of the great. Julius Caesar was persuaded by a vivid dream to cross over the Rubicon (a small river) into Italy in 49 BC, setting of civil war. It is reported that Napoleon Bonaparte used messages from his own dreams in the planning of his military victories. James Watt, one of the inventors of the steam engine, developed ball bearings thanks to a persistent series of recurring dreams. Abraham Lincoln was warned of his assassination in a dream, but chose to ignore it. Adolf Hitler, claimed that, when only a corporal in a front-line trench by the Somme during World War I, he was warned by a dream to get up and leave the bunker where he was sleeping. He did so, and very shortly afterwards the bunker was completely destroyed by an incoming shell.

*Powerful and frightening images may appear in a nightmare.*

## DREAM INTERPRETATION TECHNIQUES

If we are to stand any chance of arriving at an accurate interpretation of our dreams, there are certain techniques to be learnt in the recording, classification and de-symbolizing of our dreams.

1 While the details of a dream are usually extremely vivid and detailed as we experience them, with colour, sound and sometimes other sensory information, such details fade away rapidly on waking. By the time we have got up and had breakfast only dim outlines may remain. So it is essential to keep paper and pencil beside your bed and to write down all details immediately you wake.

2 Many dreams are clearly not foretelling the future. It could be that a simple external cause is responsible. If the bed is too warm you may dream of ovens or of sweltering under the hot desert sun. Likewise, an external noise might be integrated into your dream without being intrusive enough to wake you up. Indispositions, such as a headache or indigestion, may give rise to a particular dream, as may a television programme you have just viewed or an unusual occurrence during the day. All such simple associations, once noted, may easily be identified and the dreams eliminated as not being of the predictive kind.

3 Two other categories can also be usually be

84

ignored. Dreams early in the night are reckoned not to be predictive, and dreams full of the details of everyday existence will probably have no predictive significance. Even so, such dreams should be noted at once, for practice and for easier elimination.

Of the dreams remaining, in those containing unusual and probably predictive elements, certain motifs recur. In fact, there are a few motifs that recur in almost everybody's dreams and which have widely accepted interpretations. Here are a few examples.

**Flying** This is an image of imminent success, a sign of rising above mundane annoyances, indicating your desire to be in charge of events. But if your flying dream ends in falling this is a bad sign, suggesting insecurity, fears of failing and the strong possibility of falling out with somebody you know well.

**Hotels** This is a bad sign because of the impersonality and uniformity of hotels. Dreaming of a hotel suggests that you have a fear of being swallowed up by an organization with a consequent loss of personal identity.

**Weddings** The old belief that dreaming of a wedding is a literal prediction of a wedding in the family has largely been superseded by the

*Cats are generally omens of good luck to a dreamer.*

new, symbolic meaning of an alliance to come, most likely in the business sense although it could spell romance.

**Nakedness** While this used to be accepted as a prediction of exposure of our darkest secrets, it is nowadays thought of more as a fear of our vulnerability being exposed.

**Lakes or water** Images of water represent our emotions. Interpreting the exact message is difficult and depends partly on the state of the water in the dream. Murky water is a symbol of ill fortune. Clear, sparkling water can indicate a spiritual rebirth. Generally, water means unseen complications ahead, and it may represent the depths of and dangers from other people.

It is very important that you should not try to interpret all dreams literally. Our subconscious tends to produce symbols, puns and metaphors that cloak the meaning of dreams. Hence, a dream of a fig or fig-leaf means reference to the embarrassing parts of life, while pillars might symbolize support and a fish could stand for Christianity. Recorded puns include a horse as a warning of hoarseness, an aisle for an isle (meaning isolation), and a berry standing for burials. Oil may be a metaphor for pouring oil on troubled waters, and oats for sex.

## GOOD AND BAD OMENS

Despite what may appear to be warnings of the difficulties of trying to translate dreams into specific messages about the future, there are certain symbols whose meanings may be interpreted directly. Indications of approaching good news, luck or positive outcomes include: acorn, albatross, apricot, bazaar, broom, candle (unless flickering), castle, cat (especially black), clean or bright or shining objects, clover, earrings, flowers of most kinds, grapes, haddock, harvest, honey, hunchback, ladybird, mountain, number seven, nut, plough, rain, rice, ring, shoes, silk, singing, sky, snow, stars, sun, sunflower, thunderstorm, tiger, trees and forests (if unspoilt), turtle, uncle, walking, wine.

By contrast, bad omens, warnings, signs of bad luck or negative outcomes include: abyss, accident, ace of spades, actor or actress, alligator or crocodile, auction, barking dog, blackbird, black things, box, burn, cellar, cemetery, cliff, closed doors, comet, crab, darkness, dull or dirty object, emptiness, falcon, fighting, illness, insects, letters, marsh, meteor, mirrors, net, noise, number three, number six, party, poison, quicksand, raft, robber or burglar, sharp-edge, smoke, velvet, vulture, walls, wasp, whistle, yellow things.

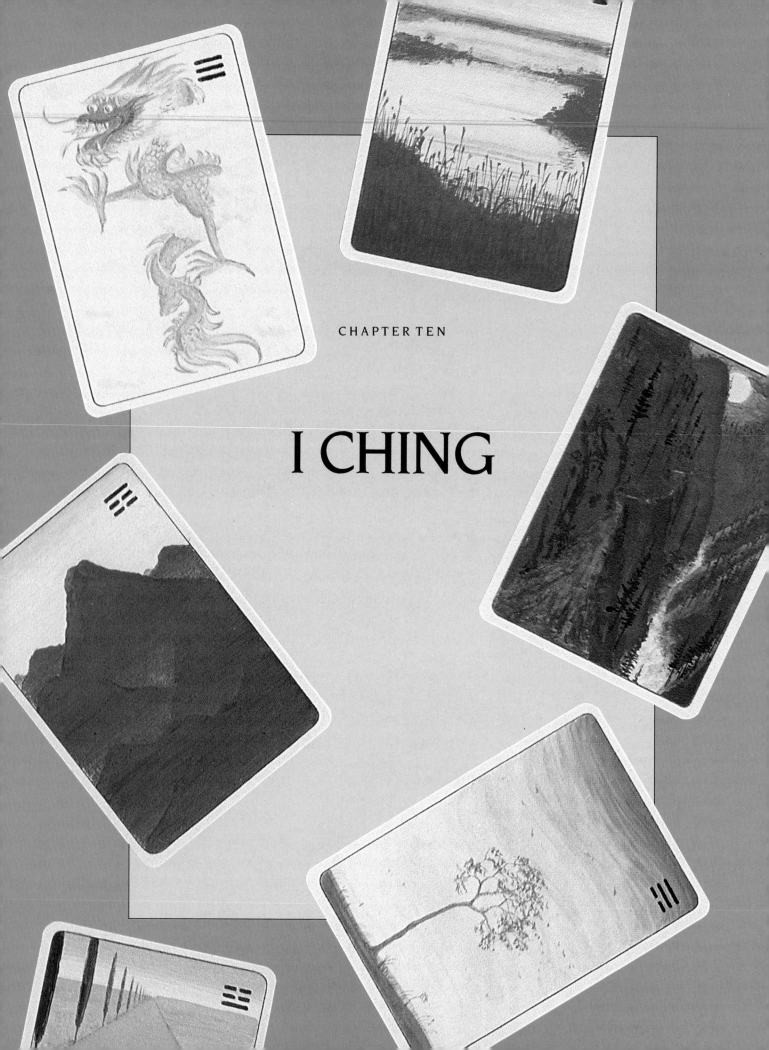

# CHAPTER TEN

# I CHING

The *I Ching* is a system of wisdom and pre-diction that is claimed to be well over 5,000 years old. It is a Chinese system that was not introduced to the West until this century, where it has come to enjoy general popularity only in the last couple of decades or so.

## YIN, YANG AND THE TRIGRAMS

The bases of the *I Ching*, which may be translated as "The Book of Changes", are the unbroken line and the broken line, and the change from one to the other.

The unbroken line is called Yang. It signifies the answer "yes", the positive, the active, the projective and traditionally the "masculine".

The broken line is called Yin. It signifies the answer "no", the negative, the passive, the receptive and the traditionally "feminine".

From these two lines, eight three-line variations are possible. These are known as the trigrams. Their invention is credited to Fu Hsi, the legendary first Emperor of China, who lived around 2,000 BC.

*The Legendary Emperor Fu Hsi is said to have invented the trigrams.*

## TRIGRAMS

| Sign | Name | Associated Image | Attributes | Family Link |
|---|---|---|---|---|
| | Ch'ien | Heaven/Sky. | Strong/powerful | Father |
| | K'un | Earth | Faithful/submissive | Mother |
| | Chen | Thunder | Impulsive/provocative | Eldest son |
| | K'an | Water/The Deep | Dangerous/flexible | Middle son |
| | Ken | Mountain | Unmoving/inevitable | Youngest son |
| | Sun | Wind/Wood/Air | Subtle/penetrating | Eldest daughter |
| | Li | Fire/Sun | Enligtening/warm | Middle daughter |
| | Tui | The Marsh/Mist/Lake | Joy/magic | Youngest daughter |

*It should be realised that there is much more complex symbolism to each of the trigrams than this.*

## HEXAGRAMS

These trigrams can be paired up in 64 combinations to produce the *I Ching* itself which consists of 64 hexagrams. Each hexagram has a very complex meaning that can be interpreted as a view of the future, or an an answer to a question or problem. The philosophical wisdom of the *I Ching* is a mixture of Taoism and Confucianism. The oracle of judgement of each hexagram is ancient and poetic. The commentary or interpretation of this is traditional and is very detailed, dealing in turn with the questioner's material prosperity and business relationships, love and friendship.

In order to get to the correct hexagram for your own question or problem or situation, you need to use a random-choice system. The systems used generate one line at a time so must be repeated six times to provide a hexagram.

There are two complications which need to be explained first. One is that the first line produced goes at the bottom of the hexagram, and each successive line is written above the previous one. The second complication is that there are not just Yang —— and Yin – – lines but Yang becoming Yin ─o─ and Yin becoming Yang ─✕─ . These last two are "moving lines" and a complete book of the *I Ching* will give readings for them in each line of each hexagram. Also, once the lines have moved (ie changed) the hexagram will be different, and that hexagram should be consulted too.

88

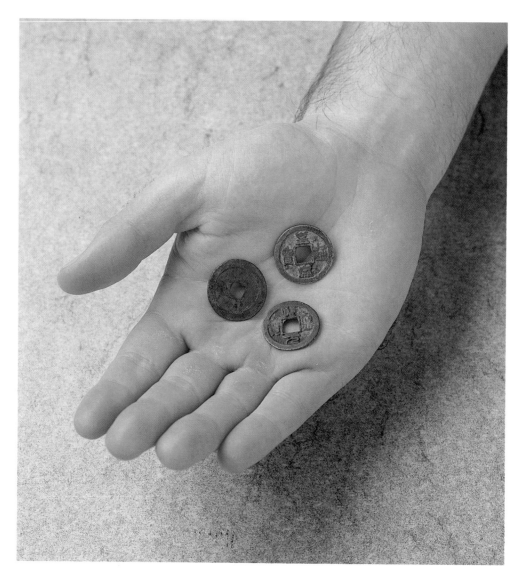

*Coins are the most commonly used way of producing hexagrams.*

*Producing hexagrams
by using yarrow
stalks is a complex
process.*

## USE OF YARROW STALKS
## OR COINS

The random-choice system can be operated
either with 49 yarrow stalks or with three coins.
Using yarrow stalks is more complex, and may
take half an hour or more, so here we will stay
with coins, which are no less traditional. The
Chinese use special coins, which are circular and
usually have square central holes, but any coins
will do. Heads are given a value of 3 and tails 2.

During the tossing of the coins, the person
wishing for an answer must keep his or her
question in mind, meditating on it. The three
coins are tossed together onto a flat surface and
the score is noted. The only possible scores are
6, 7, 8 or 9. While 7 means a normal Yang line
—— and 8 a normal Yin line — — 6 gives a
moving Yin —✗— and 9 a moving Yang —⊖—. If you
toss the coins six times, write down the score

each time (working upwards), then convert each
of the numbers to a line, you will end up with
your hexagram, such as that below.

### A HEXAGRAM EXAMPLE

| | | |
|---|---|---|
| 7 = | —— | —— |
| 7 = | —— | —— |
| 7 = | —— | —— |
| 6 = | —✗— | —— |
| 8 = | — — | — — |
| (first number) 6 = | —✗— | —— |

This is hexagram 12, which has two moving
lines. After the change it will be hexagram 13,
to the right).

The extra symbolism of the moving lines
will not be given here, but the interpretations
of hexagrams 12 and 13 can be looked up and
compared in the table following.

# TABLE OF MODERN I CHING

| 1 | 2 | 3 | 4 | 5 | 6 | 7 | 8 |
| 9 | 10 | 11 | 12 | 13 | 14 | 15 | 16 |
| 17 | 18 | 19 | 20 | 21 | 22 | 23 | 24 |
| 25 | 26 | 27 | 28 | 29 | 30 | 31 | 32 |
| 33 | 34 | 35 | 36 | 37 | 38 | 39 | 40 |
| 41 | 42 | 43 | 44 | 45 | 46 | 47 | 48 |
| 49 | 50 | 51 | 52 | 53 | 54 | 55 | 56 |
| 57 | 58 | 59 | 60 | 61 | 62 | 63 | 64 |

# SOME SIMPLIFIED INTERPRETATIONS OF THE 64 HEXAGRAMS

**1** YANG Follow the plan calmly. Do not rush. Work hard. Do not try to over-reach yourself.

**2** YIN Wait. Allow others to lead, for your happiness is in their hands. Co-operate with them.

**3** GROWING PAINS Advance very slowly and carefully. Be content with this, but ask others for guidance.

**4** YOUTHFUL IGNORANCE Find a teacher and learn to use your strength. Follow good advice. Be humble and persevere.

**5** WAITING Beware of danger. Wait and build your strength. The path will become clear. Friends will help you.

**6** CONFLICT Conflict approaches, yet it is futile. Sway with the wind; accept criticism. Wait for improvement.

**7** SOLDIERS Be ready for battle. Be organized and disciplined. You may or not need to fight. Others will help you.

**8** SEEKING UNION Work with others and peace and harmony will come. Be diligent and persevering.

**9** MINOR RESTRAINT Be restrained and sensible. Plan for hard times. Success will come later.

**10** TREADING Keep to the straight path. Walk it courageously, without hesitation or evil intent.

**11** PEACE Great gifts will come if you share your happiness. Peace comes from the powerful and weak uniting.

**12** DISJUNCTION Keep your head down during a period of stagnation, and growth will come.

**13** SOCIETY Work with others and you will emerge from obscurity. There is light for you at the end of the tunnel.

**14** WEALTH Work and study. Don't try to impress others. Don't be conceited. Support the cause of good against evil.

**15** MODESTY Humility brings power and success. Others will help if your attitude is right.

**16** ENTHUSIASM Inspire helpers with your own enthusiasm. Avoid arrogance and self-satisfaction.

**17** FOLLOWING Drift with the stream. Let others lead. Your time of success will come.

**18** FIXING Discover a problem and rectify it. Apologize if necessary. Be honest and energetic.

**19** CONDUCT Having achieved authority, be generous and cautious. Changes are coming.

**20** CONTEMPLATION Look carefully at the world around You. Be penetrative. Do not wait.

**21** BITING THROUGH Stress your virtues and achievements, however small. Ignore the jealousies of other people.

**22** BEAUTY Attractive, showy appearances are worthwhile only if they bring results. Afterwards remember to be frugal.

**23** COLLAPSE Beware of weakness and collapse. Prepare to rebuild. Guard against inside treachery.

**24** RETURNING Timing is vital. The cycle changes. Renew your energies. Watch and be patient.

**25** THE SIMPLE Be honest, simple unselfish. Do not rush in. Recognise your limitations.

**26** MAJOR RESTRAINT You have strength and power. Show restraint. Work hard. Be ready when your time for success comes.

**27** NOURISHMENT Wait and remain watchful. Practise moderation in speech and consumption. Persevere.

**28** GREATNESS IN EXCESS Know your own strength and weakness. Great changes are imminent.

**29** THE DEEP Beware of danger. Be consistent and true to yourself. Wait for the path to be revealed to you.

**30** FIRE Be intellectual and logical. Beware of burning out. Accept some dependence.

**31** TENSION Avoid all envy and excessive ambition. Be yourself. Perseverance will bring you success.

**32** CONTINUITY Avoid haste. Be casual. Occupy your space, but have a goal.

**33** RETREAT Wath out for traps and people trying to take advantage.

**34** GREAT STRENGTH Do not bluster. If you use strong words be prepared to act on them. Keep to your path.

**35** ADVANCE Effortless progress, but make sure that you are open and honest. Good fortune awaits you.

**36** DARKENING OF THE LIGHT In times of depression and gloom be cautious and flexible. Do not complain. Better times approach.

**37** THE FAMILY Deal with any problems now. Concentrate on your surroundings and family.

**38** NEUTRALITY Be flexible in small things. Reconcile any differences.

**39** DIFFICULTY Adapt to difficult circumstances. Remove or sidestep problems. Request and offer help.

**40** RELEASE Settle an acute situation quickly. Do not let yourself be held back. Advance with confidence.

**41** DECREASE Share your wealth freely with those who deserve it most.

**42** INCREASE Seize your opportunities. Accept luck but do not expect it to last.

**43** BREAKTHROUGH Watch for dangers. Ensure against them. Stay firm and thwart evil.

**44** TEMPTATION Do not be influenced by the strong. Use calm persuasion to influence other people. Caution.

**45** ACCORD If you face opposition, either go with the crowd or find an ally.

**46** PUSHING UPWARDS Great things can only be created by slow, steady growth. Keep moving upwards to your goal.

**47** REPRESSION Look into yourself to cope with a problem. Have confidence. Stay calm and continue to persevere.

**48** THE WELL Monotonous work must be done. Be generous. Watch out for tricks.

**49** REVOLUTION Watch the changing of events. Choose your moment. You will appear better to other people.

**50** THE CAULDRON Check all details. Accept small losses but work to eliminate large ones.

**51** THE THUNDERCLAP Great movement or stormy weather. Be composed and make plans.

**52** KEEPING STILL Rest and build up strength. Do not rush, gamble or take on too much. Look inwards.

**53** PROCESSION Push forwards slowly. Almost imperceptible progress is better than stagnation.

**54** THE MARRYING MAIDEN Be content with what you can get. More opportunities will come.

**55** ABUNDANCE Be inwardly happy and even in worse times you will do well.

**56** THE STRANGER You may need to travel or project yourself. Inner strength and outer modesty are both needed.

**57** THE PENETRATION OF THE WIND Gentleness and reasonableness are required. Obtain advice. Bend with the wind.

**58** PLEASURE Your strong spiritual feelings will be reflected by others. Serenity brings riches.

**59** DISPERSION Take important decisions now. Do not be inflexible or swept away. Success will come.

**60** RESTRAINT Be cautious and moderate. Do what you can in a difficult situation. Follow the rules.

**61** UNDERSTANDING Listen for warnings. Be cheerful and gentle. Endure what you must.

**62** SMALLNESS IN EXCESS Even the weak can achieve much. Avoid over-ambition. be cautious and content in yourself.

**63** COMPLETION Consolidate your success. Look forwards, but remain alert.

**64** ALMOST THERE Advance with caution. Judge carefully and take your chance.

### PHILIP K. DICK (1928-82)

The noted American science fiction writer, Philip K. Dick made unusual use of the I Ching. He consulted it and followed its advice at each stage in the plotting of his novel The Man in the High Castle (1962). It won a Hugo Award for the best science fiction novel of the year. The novel deals with an alternate world in which America, having lost World War II, has been partitioned and occupied by German and Japanese forces. The main character in the novel, a Mr Tagoni, consults the I Ching and comes to believe that this is not a true world, but a figment of the imagination.

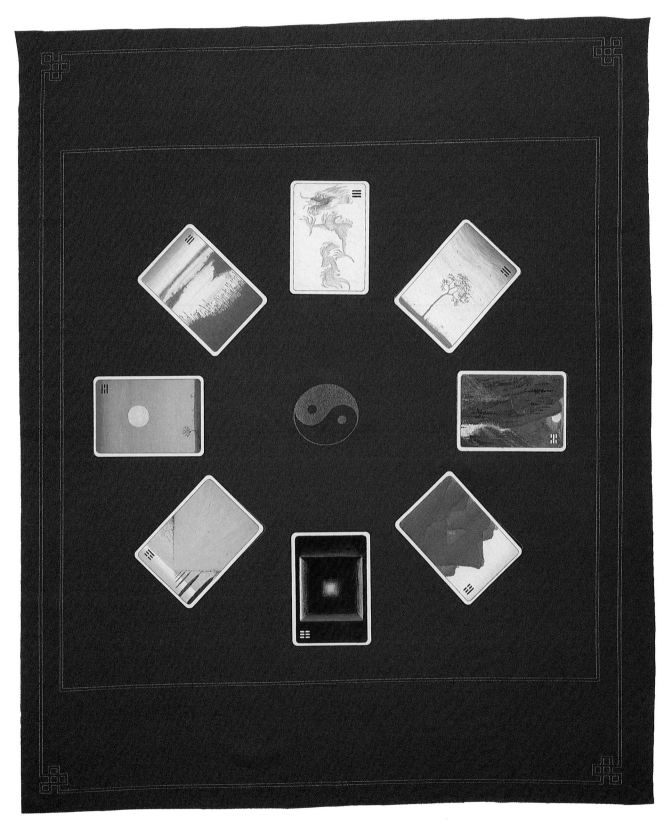

*Using cards for divination
with the I Ching is
a recent invention.*

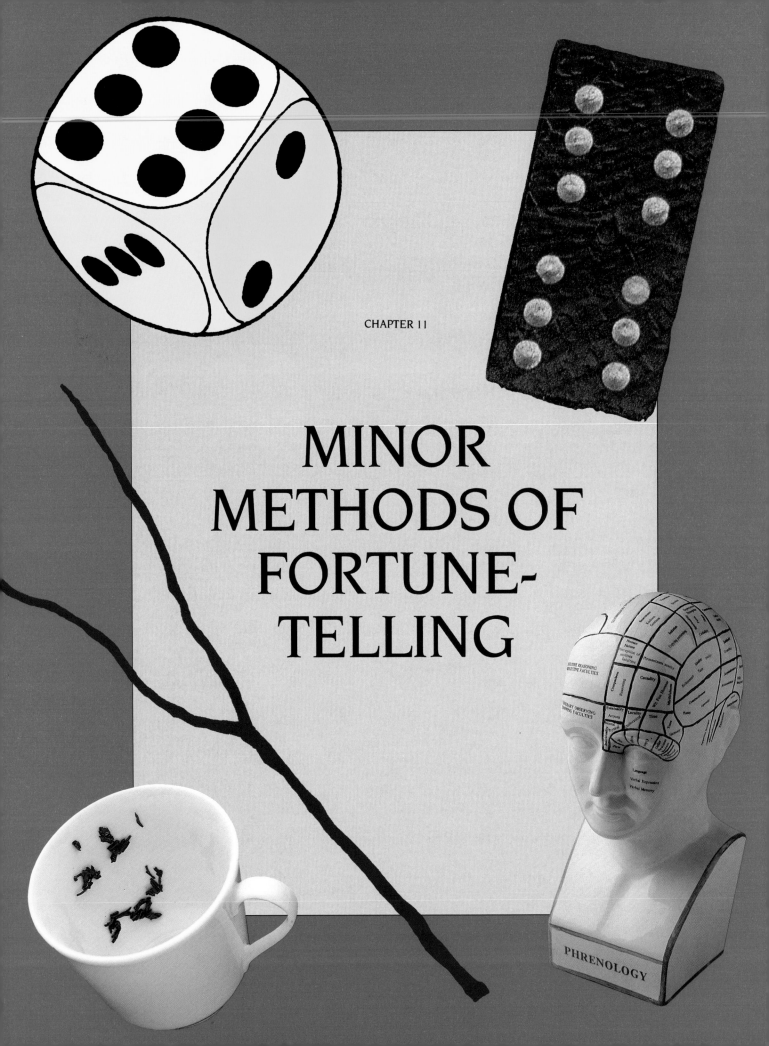

# CHAPTER 11

# MINOR METHODS OF FORTUNE-TELLING

Tasseomancy is a fancy name for divination from the patterns of tea-leaves at the bottom of a cup. It has the virtue of being a cheap and simple method of fortune-telling, with no special equipment or skills required. Probably it has been in use in the West since the seventeenth century, soon after tea became popular among Europeans. In China the practice of tasseomancy is believed to have been in existence since ancient times.

## TASSEOMANCY

There are a few simple rules. You should use a plain white teacup (not a mug), preferably broad and shallow. Any pattern or extra shape (fluting, for example) makes a reading more difficult. Do not use very fine, dusty tea, or the shape will be confusing; a large-leafed tea is best.

*Reading the tea leaves in the bottom of a cup is an old tradition.*

For the fortune to concern you, you must drink from the cup, leaving just a little liquid at the bottom, enough to cover the leaves. Then, holding the cup in your left hand, swirl the liquid gently three times in an anti-clockwise direction while thinking of a particular problem or question. Invert the cup over a saucer and leave it for a few seconds so that all the liquid drains off. When you turn the cup the right way up again, the reading can begin.

Study the leaves carefully, from different angles, for any recognizable shapes. Sometimes it is better to half-close your eyes, so that indistinct shapes achieve a little more regularity. It may be that there is nothing there, and forcing yourself to imagine a shape is no good at all. Or it may be that with careful scrutiny you can make out some object – a full moon, perhaps, or an arrow, or a ball and chain.

96

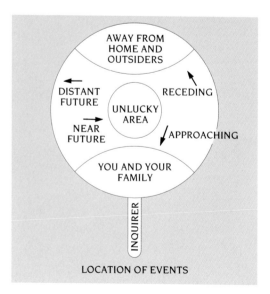

LOCATION OF EVENTS

The shapes are usually symbolic and fairly easily understood. For example, a full moon foretells a love affair, an arrow suggests imminent bad news and a ball and chain denotes unpleasant obligations. Note that all of the shapes must be read together as part of the whole fortune, not in isolation from each other.

But it is not only the shape of the leaves that is important; their position in the cup must also be noted. Because you naturally hold the cup by its handle, the handle represents you, the inquirer. Generally, the closer any shape in the leaves is to the handle, the more it will affect you (or perhaps your family). If it points away from the handle it is receding from you, and if pointing towards the handle it is approaching you. Shapes near the rim of the cup are in the present or near future, while those at the bottom of the side are still far in the future. The bottom of the cup is an unlucky area.

## USING COFFEE GROUNDS

If you are person whose does not drink tea, or who only uses tea bags, coffee grounds may be interpreted in exactly the same manner, providing you drink ground coffee, unstrained. The meanings of shapes are mostly the same as for tea, but because of the fineness of the grounds there are a few differences. For example, a triangle denotes luck coming your way, while wavy lines refer to a journey, a square means joy, and a cross foretells suffering and death in the future.

## USING MOLTEN LEAD OR WAX

An older variation of tasseomancy which is still occasionally practised is to melt a little lead or wax and drop it into cold water. The resulting shapes may be interpreted as tea-leaves. With lead this is properly known as molybdomancy and with wax as ceromancy.

In parts of continental Europe it is the custom, on New Year's Eve, to use molybdomancy in order to discover what the coming year will bring. Others hope to see the initial letter of the name of the person who they will marry formed in wax. Obviously it is safer to handle molten wax (candle wax will do) than molten lead.

## PYROMANCY

Some of the oldest forms of divination in the world involve burning. Pyromancy is an umbrella term for the various methods. It can refer to several things: judging the future from the way different substances burn (the brightness or steadiness of the flame and the presence or absence of sound); using the amount, colour and behaviour of smoke as an indicator; throwing an odd number of straws onto a red-hot surface and watching the way in which they move as they shrivel and blacken; placing marked stones in a fire as a Hallowe'en custom and inspecting their condition next morning, with an undamaged stone being a good omen for the coming year; writing a wish on a piece of paper and tossing it into a fire in a grate so that it either burns (your wish will not come true) or it is carried up the chimney by hot air (your wish will come true); looking for predictive pictures in a fire.

The last three of these are still practised today. The method for the last is to begin with a coal fire that has been burning for a while and has reduced itself to glowing, half-consumed coals. Toss a small handful of salt over the fire, then sit down in front of the fire and, once the salt has burnt off, scrutinize the embers. It is best done on one's own, in peace and quiet, preferably at night with no lights on. What you are looking for is any recognizable shape among the flaming coals.

Some of the luckiest shapes to be seen are a cat, a clover leaf, a mountain or a pair of shoes. Any kind of tree or pillar signifies an approaching love affair. An eagle, any type of flower, a hatchet or sword are unlucky omens.

## DOWSING

Traditionally, a dowser sought hidden water or mineral deposits with a divining rod, which was most often a forked twig of hazel (although a thin, pliable twig of willow, birch, apple or beech could be used just as well). These days, the dowser is more likely to have a pair of rods – plain, L-shaped wires with the shorter axis of each held loosely, and the longer axes, parallel to each other, pointing out to the front. Such rods are easily made from wire coathangers.

97

*Searching for water can be much helped by the use of dowsing.*

The system is that the dowser walks forwards holding the rods out in front of him or her, and thinking of the objective. When that objective (water, or perhaps a metal pipe) is beneath the dowser, the rods move to signify that fact. A hazel twig normally jerks up (sometimes down) quite sharply, while a pair of rods either cross or move apart. Dowsing is, of course, a form of prediction, because the dowser is predicting that a certain thing will be found at that point.

Many people possess the power to dowse in this way, and dowsing has often been used by public utility companies to locate buried water pipes or cables.

## DOWSING FOR ANSWERS

Less well known is the fact that dowsing can be used to give a "yes" or "no" answer to a wide range of questions.

The first stage (usually a matter of trial and error) is to discover, for a particular person using a particular type of rod, which reaction of the rod or rods signifies "yes" and which signifies "no". Then any question may be asked, so long as there is a clear "yes" or "no" answer. For example, if the depth of the pipe or water source is needed, specific questions must be asked about different depths. For example "is the

98

*Dowsers can locate objects using a map and a pendulum.*

water less than ten feet down?" or "is the water between ten and fifteen feet down?" and so on.

Extending this just a little, it is possible to get a person to lie down beneath the rods and to discover all sorts of information about them. For instance, "is this person aged less than 30 years?", "does this person have an IQ of more than 100?", "will this person still be alive in ten years's time?". Sometimes the rods fail to react, but with expertise and patience a detailed set of predictions may be built up.

The rods – any rods – are crude and awkward compared with a pendulum. The traditional use of a pendulum for divination was as a method of predicting the sex of an unborn child. The mother-to-be would suspend her wedding ring above her stomach by a hair from her head. If the pendulum swung in a circle the baby would be born a girl and if it swung back and forth it would be a boy. This form of divination (with a wedding ring) is known as dactylomancy.

The pendulum, however, is much more versatile than this. As with dowsing rods, its "yes" and "no" reactions need to be calibrated. Then there are no limits. Because of its small size it may be used with pinpoint accuracy. For example, it can be held over a map to predict where a pipe, a cable, a water source or even a dead body will be found. It can be asked the location of any lost object. It can be used to predict anything about the future. The only proviso is that the question must be framed so as to produce a definite "yes" or "no" answer.

Try these techniques for yourself. They are cheap, simple and may give astonishingly accurate predictions.

## SORTILEGE

Sortilege means divination by the casting of lots. Early forms of dice and marked pebbles existed in most ancient cultures; they were used for divination as well as for games.

## THROWING DICE

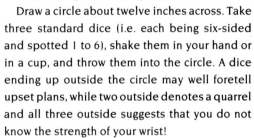

With such varied origins, it is not surprising that many different systems exist today for throwing dice and interpreting the future from the results. Here is perhaps the simplest and most widespread system, briefly described.

Draw a circle about twelve inches across. Take three standard dice (i.e. each being six-sided and spotted 1 to 6), shake them in your hand or in a cup, and throw them into the circle. A dice ending up outside the circle may well foretell upset plans, while two outside denotes a quarrel and all three outside suggests that you do not know the strength of your wrist!

The three dice, in the circle, show upper spots adding to a number from three to eighteen. Each of these totals has a meaning.

| | | | |
|---|---|---|---|
| 3 | luck, a surprise | 11 | parting or illness |
| 4 | unpleasantness | 12 | goods news |
| 5 | a wish coming true | 13 | grief |
| 6 | loss | 14 | help from a friend |
| 7 | business problems or scandal | 15 | care needed |
| | | 16 | travel |
| 8 | external influences | 17 | changing plans |
| 9 | love and marriage | 18 | great success |
| 10 | birth | | |

## USING THE CIRCLE

A refinement of this is to divide the circle into twelve equal segments, standing for different areas of your life. Moving clockwise from 12 (as on a clock) the areas are: enemies, friends, your work, your state of mind, legal things, love and marriage, health, the present, domestic items, travel, finances, next year. Each dice landing in an area may now be interpreted individually.

### SCORES

| | | | |
|---|---|---|---|
| 1 | basically good | 4 | problems |
| 2 | your success depends on others | 5 | good indications |
| | | 6 | uncertainty |
| 3 | great success | | |

## DOMINOES

Turning to dominoes, the method is to lay the set of twenty-eight face down on a flat surface and mix them. Then draw three dominoes and turn them up.

Double-six – money gained, success
Six-five – membership of an organization
Six-four – wrangles leading to a loss
Six-three – a journey, improvement
Six-two – a gift is coming
Six-one – a solution soon to your problem
Six-blank – beware of false friends
Double-five – a successful house move
Five-four – take care of a good investment
Five-three – a visit from a benefactor
Five-two – a birth
Five-one – a love affair, perhaps unhappy
Five-blank – help a friend in need
Double-four – you will attend a stranger's party
Four-three – push aside your unfounded worries
Four-two – beware a false friend
Four-one – a temporary financial setback
Four-blank – repair a torn friendship
Double-three – problems from a rival in love
Three-one – a revelation will help
Three-two – beware of bad luck for a few days
Three-blank – jealousy will mar a friendship
Double-two – you will help a happy marriage
Two-one – beware of losing a personal item
Two-blank – happiness from a new encounter
Double-one – move boldly now and you will win
One-blank – help from a stranger
Double-blank – the worst omen: loss and unhappiness

## PHRENOLOGY

Phrenology was invented in the eighteenth century by the German Dr Franz Joseph Gall. He considered that the shape of the skull reflected the shape of the brain and thus was an indication of character. Various areas of the head correspond to aspects of character, and the relative sizes of the "phrenological organs" of the head reflect particular aspects of personality. These aspects include such things as cautiousness, spirituality, mirthfulness and hopefulness. Phrenology was extremely popular during the first part of the nineteenth century; it has only a relatively small following today.

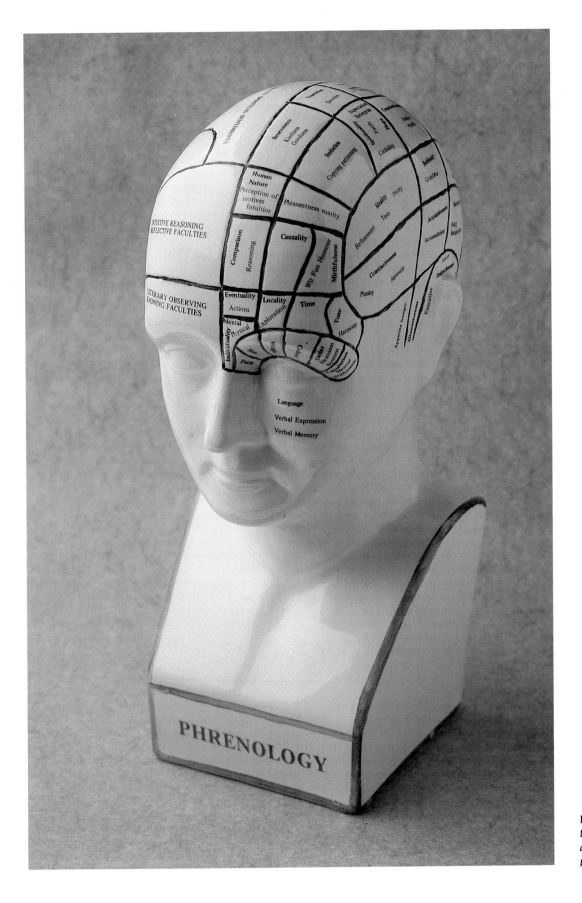

Heads marked with the regions of the skull are used by phrenologists.

CHAPTER 12

# SUPERSTITIONS

Superstitions may be ignorant and irrational beliefs in the supernatural (to paraphrase a dictionary definition) but we still take note of them. Even the hard-headed rationalist who scoffs at such things will, most likely, perform some sort of superstitious ritual every day. He may note early morning precipitation and mutter, "Rain before seven, fine before eleven". At a moment of crisis he may cross his fingers for good luck. If he finds a four-leaf clover he will be pleased, and he would think twice before walking under a ladder or opening his umbrella indoors.

## SUPERSTITIONS TRIED AND TESTED!

Some superstitions are very ancient. Many can be accounted for; to take an example, if we spill salt and toss some over our left shoulder it is because the devil is supposed to stand there, so the salt will go into his eye. A few, particularly weather predictions and medicinal remedies, have been validated by science. For example, foxglove tea was treatment for heart disease centuries before medical research showed that foxgloves contain digitalis, which is a powerful heart stimulant.

## OMENS – GOOD OR BAD?

Nearly all superstitions are omens, that is, signs of a particular future event, either good or bad. Of course, some of these future events are neither good nor bad in themselves – they may refer to weather, to the arrival of a visitor or to the identity of a husband-to-be.

Not all superstitions are old by any means. Some have sprung up in recent years, noticeably those concerned with motor vehicles. For instance, it is regarded as unlucky to buy a car painted green or a car in which somebody has died.

## A WORD OF WARNING

Generally, the power of good-luck omens is lessened or perhaps nullified if you seek them deliberately. And a lucky or unlucky appearance (such as of an animal) is only worth bothering with if the creature in question is uncommon in the area. For example, do not expect good luck (in Britain) or bad luck (in the United States) every time a black cat crosses your path if the cat is your own pet.

# A CATALOGUE OF SUPERSTITIONS

## BIRTH AND CHILDHOOD

### UNLUCKY OMENS

- Anticipating the sex of a baby.
- Taking a pram into the house before the birth.

### LUCKY OMENS

- The baby is born on a Sunday (this is the most fortunated day on which to be born).
- A baby born with a caul (this is very lucky).
- A baby born with an open hand will be generous in later life.
- For a baby to cry at its christening is lucky, because this means that any evil spirits are leaving its body.

In the United States, a baby is still occasionally offered a Bible and a bottle of whisky. If the baby reaches for the Bible, it will be God-fearing (and perhaps enter the Church). If it reaches for the bottle there is no hope for it.

If one twin dies at birth, the other will soon follow because they share a soul. Alternatively, the other inherits its dead sibling's strength. Take your pick!

*A horseshoe brings luck to a house, and St Christopher to a traveller.*

## IN THE HOME

- If you drop a spoon, a visitor is to be expected.
- If you drop a fork, the visitor will be female.
- If you drop a knife, you will receive a male visitor.
- If two women pour coffee or tea from the same pot, one of the two will be pregnant before the end of the year.

### BAD LUCK OMENS

- Forgetting to put the lid on a coffee-pot or teapot before pouring means that a stranger is coming with bad news.
- If you break a cup you can expect to break two more the same day (breakages are supposed to go in threes – like many other bad-luck and good-luck occurrences). The only remedy is to break the heads off two matches.
- Leaving Christmas decorations up in the house after Twelfth Night.
- Putting your left shoe on before your right.
- Taking eggs into or out of the house during the hours of darkness.
- Bringing lilac, may blossom or a sprig of broom into the house.
- A bat flying into the house.
- Having peacock feathers around the house (this is very unlucky).
- Breaking a mirror in the house gives seven years'

*One cup is broken: two more cups will break subsequently.*

*If one horseshoe brings luck, what must many bring to a household?*

bad luck. This is based on the belief that the human body renews itself every seven years and therefore it will take that long for all of the bad luck to disappear.

**PRECAUTIONS TO TAKE IN THE HOME FOR GOOD LUCK**
- Nail a horseshoe to the door of your house (so long as the ends point upwards).
- Sneeze three times before breakfast.
- Spill your drink when you propose a toast.
- Spill a box of matches.

## IN THE STREET

**LUCKY OMENS**
- Meeting the same person by chance twice while you are out on business (which is a particularly lucky omen).
- A strange dog following you home.
- Picking up a pencil in the street.

**UNLUCKY OMENS**
- Meeting a grave-digger.
- Dropping your umbrella.

## BIRDS AND OTHER ANIMALS

There are so many omens connected with birds that divination by this means has its own name, ornithomancy. Here are just a few of the omens.

### LUCKY BIRD OMENS

- Seeing white birds, or birds, to your right.
- Seeing birds approaching (the greater the flying height, the greater the good fortune).
- Seeing a dove, peacock, robin, swallow, or woodpecker.
- A gull landing on any ship you are travelling in.

### UNLUCKY BIRD OMENS

- Seeing dark birds or birds seen to your left.
- Birds flying away from you (they take luck away with them).
- A gull brushing against you with its wings; this is an omen of death.

106

*Bad luck comes into the house with peacock feathers.*

- Magpies are, in general, unlucky birds, although the omen relies on the number seen, as in the old rhyme:

> One's sorrow, two's mirth,
> Three's a wedding, four's a birth,
> Five's a christening, six a dearth,
> Seven's heaven, eight is hell,
> And nine's the Devil his ane sel.

(*ane sel* = own self)

### LUCKY ANIMAL OMENS

- Meeting a goat, a piebald horse or a flock of sheep.

### UNLUCKY ANIMAL OMENS

- Hearing a bat squeaking as it flies overhead.
- Meeting a hare (especially if you are a sailor on your way to your ship).
- Seeing a black rat.
- Encountering any kind of reptile (except a tortoise or turtle).

*Bees are generally looked on as being lucky insects.*

## INSECTS AND SPIDERS

It is widely believed (even among bee-keepers) that bee stings prevent rheumatism.

Despite the common phobia of spiders, few people will kill one, perhaps because of this rhyme.

> *If you wish to live and thrive,*
> *Let a spider run alive.*

### GOOD OMENS

- Seeing a white butterfly.
- Hearing crickets.
- Finding a ladybird (ladybug), especially one with seven black spots, for obvious numerological reasons.
- Receiving a hive of bees as a gift.
- Catching and keeping a bee briefly before releasing it unharmed. Finding a small (money) spider on your clothes or on your body. Watching a spider cross a wall or climb its thread.

*Bad luck may befall if you see three butterflies together.*

**BAD OMENS**

- Seeing three butterflies together.
- Being bitten by an ant (it means enmity and quarrels to come).
- Encountering a cockroach.
- Being stung by a wasp (it brings jealousy, deception and danger).
- Killing a cricket or spider.
- Seeing a spider drop to the floor.

## WEATHER

Every kind of weather brings a different omen. Many of these weather superstitions are ancient and reinforced by rhymes. "March dry, good rye. March wet, good wheat." was an optimistic farmers' saying.

A shorter-term prophecy was, "A fine Saturday, a fine Sunday, a fine week."

### RAIN OMENS

The most vital ingredient of weather (for the farmers, at least) was rain, so hundreds of rain omens exist. For example, any rain falling on St Swithin's Day (July 15) is meant to preface 40 more consecutive days of rain. Another rain rhyme goes like this:

*If the oak is out before the ash,*
*We shall only have a splash.*
*But if the ash is out before the oak,*
*We shall have a real soak.*

*A red sky in the evening may tell that you will not need an umbrella.*

108

Other common omens of impending rain
- Cattle lying down.
- A red sky in the morning.
- Cocks crowing at nightfall.
- A cuckoo calling persistently.
- Jackdaws fluttering around buildings.
- A cat sneezing.
- A halo around the Moon.
- Itching corns.

**UNITED STATES RAIN OMENS**
- Horses clustering in a corner of their field.
- The cawing of crows.
- Fish biting more enthusiastically in streams.
- Moles throwing up more hills than normal.
- Bees staying in their hive.
- Frogs croaking and donkeys braying excessively.
- Swallows flying low.
- Pigeons circling over water.
- Turkeys taking dust-baths.

**WHAT YOU CAN DO TO CAUSE RAIN**
- Step on a black beetle, a spider or an ant.
- Cut ferns.
- Sprinkle water onto stones.
- Throw flour into a spring and stir with a hazel stick (an old French ritual).

## AT WORK

In jobs and professions where there are close-knit communities, superstitions abound.

**BAD LUCK AT SEA**
- Stepping on or off ship left foot first.
- Pets on a ship are generally unlucky.
- A corpse on board is very unlucky. If a corpse is carried in to port, it must leave the ship before any living person.
- Cut your nails or hair at sea during a calm could raise a gale.
- A sailor does not whistle because it may summon up the devil.

**DOWN THE MINES**
Miners have many superstitions, including the belief that whistling down the mine brings bad luck.

**BAD LUCK IN THE THEATRE**
- Whistling.
- Saying the last line of a play in rehearsal.
- Having a perfect final rehearsal.
- Wishing an actor good luck (so actors usually say, "break a leg").
- Referring to Shakespeare's Macbeth by name (actors call it "the Scottish play").

## ROMANCE AND MARRIAGE

There are superstitions covering every aspect of love and marriage, from the best occasion for sweethearts to kiss for the first time (by the light of a new moon), through tests of constancy and warnings against being photographed together before the wedding, right down to the details of the wedding day itself. Wednesday is the best day to marry, and meeting a chimney sweep (rare these days) is good luck. Meeting a pig on your wedding day means ill fortune.

Do young women still go to great lengths to catch a supernatural glimpse of their future husbands? Perhaps not, although the instructions still exist.

*Point your shoes towards the street,*
*Tie your garters around your feet,*
*Put your stockings under your bed,*
*And you'll dream of the man you're going to wed.*

Another ritual should be carried out on Hallowe'en night. The young woman must go to her room and light two candles on her dressing table. Then, standing silently in front of her mirror, she must brush her hair and eat an apple. The visage of her future husband will be seen in the glass, looking over her shoulder.

## FOOD

- If you sleep with wedding cake under your pillow, you should dream of your future partner.
- Fasten various possible answers to a question each on to one of several onions. Plant the onions and wait to see which sprouts first; the answer is attached to this onion.
- An egg white may be put into a wine glass partly full of water and lightly shaken. The shapes formed can be read as if they were tea-leaves.
- If you drop an egg accidentally and it breaks, this foretells good news; if the egg does not break, beware of bad tidings.
- When cutting a loaf of bread, take care to do so evenly, for a ragged or uneven slice is a sure sign that the person cutting has been telling lies.
- Eating carrots produces good eyesight.
- Eating fish helps the brain.

## DEATH

It is very unlucky to enter a house through the back door and leave it by the front, because this was the route used by funerals.

When somebody dies, the clocks in the house should be stopped, curtains drawn and mirrors covered over.

There are no omens of good luck connected with death, perhaps not surprisingly.

## OMENS OF DEATH

*If dropped scissors stick into the floor, a death is foretold.*

- Scissors falling and coming to rest point down.
- A raven flying to your left and calling.
- A single magpie to your left.
- Magpies flying past a house (death to somebody in the house).
- A dog howling outside your house.
- A black beetle running over your shoe.
- Seeing a cockroach in an unusual place.
- When you hear of one death you will soon hear of another one.

# INDEX

*Page numbers in italics refer to illustrations.*

110

112

# ACKNOWLEDGEMENTS

The publishers would like to thank the following for the pictures on the pages listed (T = top, B = bottom, L = left, R = right).

Chris Morgan 106R, 107.
E. T. Archive 73, 82.
Images Colour Library 10, 13, 14, 20, 47, 53, 55, 57, 72, 81, 84, 85, 87, 89, 90, 95, 97, 105, 106L, 108.
Joel Finler 27, 28, 32.
The Jung Society 83.
Nicole Olivien Panter 92.
Pictorial Press 23, 26, 29, 30, 31, 33, 34, 35, 36, 37, 68B&T.
All other photographs were taken by Martin Norris.

The author would like to thank the following people for advice and providing materials.

Shirley Cooper
Do Walsh
Eileen Appleby
Rog and Arline Peyton
Lynn Edwards
And his wife, Pauline, ever helpful with constructive criticism and tarot readings.